Divine.
messy.
HUMAN.

Divine. Messy. Human.

∞

A Spiritual Guide to Prioritising
Internal Truth over External Influence

∞

Amanda Kate

Copyright © 2022 by Amanda Kate
www.amandakate.com.au

Editor: Ruth Fae from Fae Blood Publications
Cover by: Clare Blackstock from Blade Creative

First Printing, 2022
ISBN 978-0-6453481-1-8

Disclaimer: This book contains stories from the perspective of my truth. People from my past will have different truths of who I was, who I am from their own point of truth, and their memory of the situations, interactions and stories within this book. I respect their truth and do not deny their perspectives of their truth. And I also honour mine.

In order to maintain anonymity, names and gender are not included and some identifying characteristics have been changed. The information, views and opinions are solely those of the author and publisher. The author and publisher disclaims any liabilities or responsibilities whatsoever for any damages, libel and liabilities arising directly or indirectly from the contents of this publication.

This book is not intended as a substitute for the medical advice of physicians. The reader should regularly consult a physician in matters relating to his/her health and particularly with respect to any symptoms that may require diagnosis or medical attention, including any mental health concerns.

All rights reserved. No part of this book may be reproduced in any manner whatsoever without written permission except in the case of brief quotations embodied in critical articles and reviews appropriately credited to the author.

Note: Throughout this book, I make a distinction between self and Self.
    - 'self' indicates the egoic self, the attachment to our personality and the unawakened conscious mind
    - 'Self' indicates the Higher Self, the unconscious mind, the wise part of us which is connected to the All That Is
You will also notice capitalisation of other words, such as 'Higher Self' or 'Divine Self', to indicate the higher connection we make when we are more present, aware and embodied.

My Reasons for Doing the Things

To my twin flame, life partner and love, BJ. Thank you for being in my life, for being my shield when I need to retreat from the world, for challenging me in the most wonderful way and for loving me, not despite my flaws, but because of them. You make my life brighter as you stand at my side.

To my children, everything I have done was through love for you. That love kept me going when I wanted to give in to the darkness and saw me through the other side of my dark nights into the light at the end of the tunnel. I love you both to the moon and back and am forever grateful for your presence in my heart.

I would like to pay my respects and give thanks and gratitude to all those who have hurt me. I know in return, or initiation, I have hurt you too and for that I am sorry. I have learned my lessons and used this as fuel for my personal growth and development, taking full responsibility for my part in what played out.

I am sorry
Please forgive me
Thank you
I love you

I would also like to pay my respects to the past, present and emerging Traditional Custodians and Elders of Australia, and I wish to acknowledge them as Traditional Owners.

Contents

My Reasons for Doing the Things v

Divine, Messy and Human 1
    Curiosity and Questions 4
    What is my Understanding of Spirituality? 6
        Journal Prompts 9

What is 'Wholing' and Why is it Different from Healing? 10

From Oneness to Individuality 14

Creating Golden Opportunity from Leaden Experience 18

The Truth has 144 Sides 21

Negative Thoughts and our Propensity for Darkness 26
    Sleepwalking through Life 28
        Journal Prompts 30

The Power of Language within Healing 32
    Letting Go 34
    The Words you Use 36
    Affirmations 38

Baby Steps 41

From Selfless or Selfish to Self-Full 44

You are not Broken 47

Don't let that C**t Steal your Bricks 50
    We all have C**ts who try to Diminish us 55

When Friends Speak Up 57

External Influence 59

The Inner Self versus the Outer Self 64
    What is your Reality? 67
    This is Me 70

What is Trauma? 71
    Fight, Flight, Freeze, Fragmentation, Fawn 74
    Comparative Suffering 75
    Moving towards Desire 77

My Best is Good Enough 79

The Three-Legged Stool 84

Emotional Fluency 88
    Mad, Sad and Glad 90
    The Paradox of Conflicting Emotions 98
        Exercises: Building Emotional Fluency 101
        Feeling Emotional Weight 101
        Acknowledge and Validate > Shift or Stay? 102
        Journal Prompts 103

Self-Love: Gritty and Real 104

Boundaries 108
        Exercise: Creating Boundaries 110
        Saying a Divine No 110
    Self-Talk 112
        Exercise: Access your Inner Wise Person, Best Friend and
        Encouragers 117
        Exercise: Monitor your Internal Voice 119
    'In Service To' versus 'Of Service To' 120
    Cultivating Self-compassion, Acceptance and Honesty 123
    Energetic Currency + Discernment = Self-Love 125
    Relationships 128
    What do you WANT and NEED? 131
        Journal Prompts 135

Balancing Opposing Principles 136

Goals versus Desires 139
Giving and Receiving 144
    Exercise: Meet your Masculine and Feminine 147
Holding the Tension of Opposite Forces 149

Living the Spiritual Paradox 152
    Creativity, Humour, and the Spiritual Path 155

Discerning your Soul's Intuitive Whispers 162
    How do we Access our Insight and Intuition? 166
    Clairvoyance 167
    Clairaudience 169
    Clairsentience 170
    Claircognizance 170
    Clairsaliance and Clairgustance 171
    Spirit Guides, Totems and Higher Realm Beings 172

Now for the Dirtiest Word in the Book: Self-Responsibility 175
    Bringing your Work into Grounded Reality 179
        Exercise: Connecting to Earth and Heavens 180

What's Next? 182
    Acknowledgements 187
    Bibliography and Webography 191

Divine, Messy and Human

This book is for the messily human, the ones who are trying their best and making mistakes. It is for those who want to embrace their messiness and learn to love it, realising life gives us all lessons we need to learn.

It is when things are against us that we feel the greatest test and challenge to our spiritual beliefs. And, sometimes, there aren't enough incense sticks, yoga poses, deep breaths or positive affirmations to ward away the darkness and reconnect to our inner light. We need to dig deep to find the God source connection that creates our safe harbour within the tempest of the storm.

This is where regular practice comes in. The ability to gather 'knowingness' and trust in the Universe. To anchor into our heart and soul knowing that, even in the tempestuousness, there are learnings, lessons and growth, if we care to look and feel within.

When shadows appear, the tests and trials can feel painfully raw, insurmountable, too much, and overwhelming.

I've experienced loud *'I'm done!'* days when the easier choice would be to stay in bed, give up and let the demons come and take me away. Those times continue to surprise me with their unexpected presence, usually just when I feel that I've got my shit together. Such is the rollercoaster of life.

But, the way to peace and light is through the darkness. When we feel that the light at the end of the tunnel will never appear, we often glimpse a flicker in the distance, giving us hope that we will reach that place of inner peace and greater illumination.

In these pages, I share with you some of the darkness I've encountered, and how I've found the light within those moments when I never thought I'd see it again. These practices are the heart and soul of my journey of self-discovery. They are the tools and techniques I've used, and continue to use, to turn my life around and alchemise self-hatred and loathing into self-empowerment, self-love, liberation, abundance and freedom.

Freedom from the expectation to be who I perceived everybody wanted me to be, the person I busted my arse trying to become, to the woman I've felt bubbling in my heart and soul daily beneath the conditioning. The one I was too afraid to let out into the light.

I am still messy and human. I cuss and swear, and I live a spiritual life.

Living a spiritual life is not about moving to a Tibetan mountain top and meditating day in, day out for the rest of our lives. That may work for a set period of time, (let's face it, a seven day retreat would be divine every now and then), but the challenge for most of us is to sprinkle our spiritual practice throughout the day like nourishing raindrops of soul food.

Access the peace in as many moments as you can. Find the balance between living a full human life experiencing the range of emotions - joy and sorrow, connection and loneliness, love and hurt - and learning to be ok, no matter the emotional state within and around us, through our connection to something greater.

To experience the full richness of our time here on Earth, our spiritual existence must be balanced between human needs and foibles, and spiritual joy. We have to find a way to bring our spiritual Self into our mundane daily tasks without checking out of reality and life responsibilities. To be present in each moment and find magic in the monotony.

Once I began working in the healing arts, I didn't want to add stress to my life, or to my clients' lives, by using complicated, ritualistic tools. Initially, I felt overwhelmed because, by the time I'd done all the spiritual practices I'd been taught, half the day was over. So I took complicated practices I'd learned, and simplified them to fit into the gaps I had made in my day to work on my self and spiritual development.

The best way to build up spiritual practice is through small, incremental daily habits.

Learning to slot techniques into gaps in my day took the pressure off. I prioritised those practices that give me the most 'bang for my buck' and made them non-negotiable, then included the ones which are lovely, yet more time consuming, as part of my ritual work and ad hoc practice.

In this book, I share my first-hand experience of the techniques, practices and knowledge that I use to create a lived wisdom that increases my abundance in love and life.

My hope is that you will flip through these pages, scribble notes in the margins, and use these practices, whether life is going well or throwing you a curveball. The more you work with these techniques, the more innately integrated and easily recalled they will be when the going does, inevitably, get tough.

Curiosity and Questions

If you feel drawn to, please use the questions and exercises as journal or reflection prompts. While writing is a great practice, it's not for everyone. I tend to process my questions on my daily walks, only using a journal when I am truly drawn to put words on a page. You will process your curiosity in the way that is best for you. If you don't yet know what that is, then play with the concept - write in a journal, think while on a walk or run, ruminate on the prompts in a bath. Whatever you are drawn to is perfect for you. We do not walk a 'one size fits all' path.

We won't always find answers to every question. Some questions will only lead to more questions, which lead to 'awarenesses', which lead to questions. There is no end point to our digging and delving if we wish to work on healing all levels of our being.

Bring out your 'inner toddler' and allow them to ask you *'Why?'* until they are blue in the face.

Create fun answers and don't be afraid to let

questions hang in the ether.

Often the questions we can't answer ourselves find their solutions via some intervention of Divine Godliness, in ways we couldn't expect in our wildest dreams.

Since my breakdown/falling apart/unravelling/coming together/awakening, (it has many guises and facets, and continues to this day), I have looked to find the simplest strategies to live a wholehearted life.

I ask you to bring in your playfulness, sense of humour, grace, and curiosity as you traverse these pages and explore how to awaken to new ways of being, responding and communing with others. Be curious with what I offer here and see what fits you and your routine, as well as the calling of your soul.

As you read, connect deeply with the knowingness within you. Understand that *right now* you are exactly where you need to be on your path. Whether you have been walking it for a while, are just starting out, or have merely caught a glimpse of others and wondered what the hell they're doing, know that, at this moment, you are perfectly placed on your journey.

We are all works in progress. As we go deeper within and uncover more layers to transform and transmute, we evolve and ascend to new levels of consciousness, awareness and understanding.

I write this book from my level of experience, awareness and consciousness as it is, now, at this moment. I will continue to evolve as I peel back layers, unlearn deeply conditioned programming and ideologies, relearn new ways of being, and understand how to embody them in this manifest reality. Then I will be at my next level of growth, awareness and understanding to repeat the process once again.

Even as we traverse the path of self-development, personal growth and budding alchemy, we will trip up, make mistakes and revisit old, less-than-beneficial patterns in reaction to our triggers.

In moments such as these, the key is self-compassion.

Know that you are doing the best you can in any given moment, and that you will continue to learn on your path to growth.

What is my Understanding of Spirituality?

Spirituality means so many things to so many people. I define my understanding here, not to influence you, but so you are clear on what I mean when I use the term. Please give yourself the meaning that speaks to you and substitute the words I use for 'power greater than our human self' to a word or words that resonate and give greatest meaning to you.

I figure there must be a power higher than our 'self' because, let's face it, if we are in control of all this, then I think we're in trouble. The existence of a Higher Power takes the pressure off us to be perfect, have our shit together all the time, and know fully what's going on.

My perception of Spirituality is my own personal relationship with the Higher Power that sits above the humans of this world - *Goddess, God, Source, The Universe, Divine Intelligence, The One, Nature, Super Conscious,*

Supreme Intelligence, Life Force. Call it what you will, for me, those terms are one and the same. It is not about the name we give to something, but the feeling it evokes in us.

All of these are purity embodied - pure love, joy, happiness, connection, union, oneness, peace, flow, acceptance, non-judgement.

For me, they do not symbolise idols to worship, doctrines to immerse in, or dogmas to follow, but embody states of being and mindsets to engage with and get to know on a deep, cellular level. They show us a path to connect with fellow humans, other sentient beings, and our natural environment, in a way where we step lightly and leave little evidence of our having been there except for love, compassion and care.

I can tell you, truthfully from my heart and soul, that it has taken years of healing, therapy and delving into past traumas and pain to feel connected to the word 'God'.

For years, I avoided that word like it was poisonous and, in some way, dirty. Now that I have healed the underlying traumas, that word sits high on my list of how to describe the energy of the feelings I embody within my own sense of spirituality.

'*God*' was tainted by religious doctrine, dogma and idol worship. Some of the most religious people in my sphere were hypocritical beyond belief. I passionately hated the hypocrisy as I sat in church with people who pretended to be holier-than-thou, then watched them walk out of the building to be exactly the same arsehole they were before they walked in. They professed faith, love and compassion, yet displayed judgement, nastiness and hatred. It took time, love, self-compassion, and a lot of healing, to see that they were only human beings doing the best they could with the tools they had. They didn't know any better and their intention was certainly not to consciously taint God's name for me or anyone else.

God remains ungendered for me - neither masculine nor feminine. They are not the patriarchal, fire and brimstone, wrathful and vengeful God, but a God of love, compassion and grace for all children of the earth.

The God I know and have experienced shows grace and acceptance, holds us in our darkness, and smiles at our light. They are the ever-loving, non-judgemental parent who wants what's best for us and loves us regardless.

Living a spiritual life isn't about denying reality and living in a world of only love and light, sunshine and roses, rainbows, unicorn farts and perfection.
It is about accepting life and humanness in all its messy reality.

Ups, downs and days when we just feel 'meh'.

We cycle continuously through stages of learning. We birth new projects and events into the world, then move into the death cycle where things come to completion and we ready ourselves for the next cyclical movement.

Humans are energy in motion. We are in a constant state of flux, balance and change. As we develop our spiritual nature and reconnect with our heart, soul and true Self, we learn to honour the cycles, engage in greater alignment of our truth, and connect in deeper levels to those around us, Universal Consciousness, and Nature.

The spiritual path is about embracing our light and our dark, positives and negatives, being honest with ourselves, and learning to love all aspects of ourselves without judgement - to bring the fullness of who and what we are as Self into the fold of our humanity.

Through my own personal experience of spirituality, I have found greater openness, honesty and peace with Self and others. I have come to a calm forgiveness for past hurts and, more importantly, have turned that forgiveness towards myself with compassion for doing the best I could in any given moment, with the tools I had available to me at the time.

During your journey, I ask you to make friends with your understanding of spirituality.

Journal Prompts

What does Spirituality mean to you?

What does a spiritual relationship with your Divine Source look like/feel like?

How do you feel God? In what places and moments do you just know God is with you - nature, church, garden, heart, within, without, listening to music, dancing?

What is 'Wholing' and Why is it Different from Healing?

'Wholing' is a term I first came across in Sol Luckman's book Potentiate your DNA. *It speaks to the way I see, think and feel about the healing process, particularly since I found natural healing and the wide range of modalities that work with the mind-body-spirit.* Luckman explains:

>   Healing (wholing) must not be confused with simple curing… Curing is designed to make the problem go away, no questions asked and no insights gained, healing is a very different activity.
>   True healing embraces the problem (which is actually a teaching tool employed by our Higher Self) as a way of integrating and being transformed by it.
>   Curing focuses on symptoms without realising they are spiritual messages…. healing is a body-mind-spirit phenomenon involving an increase in awareness that takes the form of a transformational step on our evolutionary journey of conscious personal mastery.

Boom!

The healing journey is about going back and picking up all the pieces of self that we have suppressed, repressed, oppressed, hidden away and cut off ourselves due to shame, embarrassment, trauma or other life events.

Subconsciously, we hide parts of ourselves to ensure that we 'fit in' and can be embraced by our tribe, but often do ourselves a disservice by not showing others, or acknowledging to ourselves, the True light of our Being.

Before walking this path, I had chronic fatigue, the beginning of an autoimmune picture, suffered over 13 days a month with my menstrual cycle, experienced adrenal fatigue, and was physically, mentally and emotionally falling apart. The exhaustion was overwhelming and it became hard to cope with normal life. Despite blood tests and numerous doctors appointments, the traditional Western style of medicine could find nothing wrong with me. They attempted to put me on antidepressants, but I knew deep down that was not the problem.

My life changed for the better when natural medicine and modalities came into my sphere of awareness.

Not once in all the years had Western GPs and doctors done anything other than look at blood tests and try to push pharmaceuticals. Now, I was being asked key questions about my support structures, relationships, and emotional, mental and physical well-being.

Finally dealing with the true issues causing the physical manifestation of illness, I not only recognised the lack of support in my life, but registered on a conscious level that my soul was miserable, out of alignment, hungering for change and desperate to feel desire for life again. I craved happiness, connection and something greater than a life that looked good on paper. I wanted to feel goodness in my life.

When explaining the healing journey to a client, I received an image from my Spirit Team. They showed me that 'wholing' is a little like clearing the muck from the shower drain. The hair used to be smooth, straight, healthy and attached to us. With trauma, daily life and stress, that hair becomes damaged, breaks off and finds its way to meld and mix with other substances in a big, grand, messy old tangle.

As we walk the healing path, we begin to untangle that hair, clean it off, remove the grime and muck, and comb it out, allowing us to recreate the strands and make sense of the entanglements. The tangle becomes clean, brushed straight and lovingly restored. We learn to love those parts of us, remember the gift they were and how it helped us along our journey.

A bit gross, but my Spirit Team do have a sense of humour. They give me visuals that are impactful, often funny, and help lighten the mood within deep healing settings which can be very serious and teary. Laughter is, after all, the best medicine.

As we examine and begin to understand lessons, learnings and growth behind why we've rejected certain parts of ourselves, and why they cause us pain, imbalance and a lack of wellness, we can learn to love those pieces, light or dark, and lovingly bring them back into the fold of our being.

We heal through the process, but also become more whole and more congruent with our heart and soul.

Alchemy is transformation and transmutation. As we take those vibrational changes, they filter down to a cellular level, to create golden opportunities where there once was lead. The process allows the light both in and out, and creates expansion for growth.

This is the true grace, magic, awe and wonder of the path we walk as we become more whole and aligned with our True Self and Divine Nature.

From Oneness to Individuality

When we are born into this world, we come from the All That Is, the Oneness of the Universe, our God-Source. We are pure love, acceptance, compassion, joy and spirit. We are One with everything, undifferentiated and energetic beings.

I imagine that we exist like air in a house. Who's to say where the kitchen air becomes the lounge or dining room air? We all overlap and intermingle in a wondrous, high energy existence of purity.

When we come into our Earthly body, we choose to come into individual existence and learn the lessons that such an existence will give us to enhance our understanding, dimensionality and wisdom.

With conception, we choose to leave the Higher Realms and begin the process of embodiment into this dimension, the Earth realm and human consciousness.

Women are born with all the eggs that they have for their lifetime. So, when we arrive in the human womb as a soul, choosing to incarnate with that particular mother and father, we also choose to incarnate with the lessons passed down from generations before.

Our DNA holds the conditioning of our Grandmother from the time our mother's eggs are fully formed in her womb, until our mother and her mother separate their energy fields, as well as from our mother from the time she is born until we separate our energy fields from her. That's a lot of paraphernalia to carry into this world.

We also come in with the lessons we need to learn in this lifetime, and any karmic contracts and behaviours from previous lifetimes that feed into what we are here to learn and embody to aid our ascension.

Until we reach approximately the age of 7, we remain part of our mother's energy field and don't have full conscious awareness of our actions, responsibility, consequences and the more mature concepts we learn as we grow. But when children hit the age of 7-8, they go through what I lovingly call 'the arsehole phase'. They push boundaries as they try to learn where they energetically end and others begin, and they separate from their mother's energy to become their own individual being. While they process that shift, it's as though they need to 'act out', misbehave and not listen, in order to receive the feedback that shows them the acceptable boundaries for their behaviour.

This process of individuation from purity of spirit to human comes with complications.

We learn acceptable and non-acceptable behaviours from the adults around us, not only by what they say, but also by what their actions show us. We develop belief systems around what we need to do to fit into the prescribed parameters and, when we deeply believe that our conduct is unbecoming, we create defence mechanisms, reactions and other safety measures to adjust our behaviour so that we will not be 'thrown out of the tribe'.

Our brains are still quite undeveloped in many ways. The deep, underlying belief pattern that sits as root cause beneath all others is that:

If we are rejected from the community, we will be cast out into the wilderness, and we will die.

'Fitting in' is imperative to feel that we are secure within our group and will be able to progress to adulthood.
Our Reticular Activating System (RAS) is part of the physiology that supports this learning of behaviour and reactionary patterns.

The RAS is a part of the brain that helps us focus on and filter the elements of incoming information we need to anchor ourselves to. When we assign importance to something and heighten its value in our life, the RAS looks for examples to back up our belief.

For example, before I was pregnant, I rarely noticed pregnant people anywhere. Once pregnant with my first child, it seemed that every second woman I saw was pregnant - because I had assigned greater importance to pregnancy. This also works with bringing information into our awareness to back up our negative belief systems. If we decide, for example, that we are a failure, we unconsciously search for information and statistics to back up that underlying belief structure and prove our case.

As we get older, if we're lucky, we start to find that our behaviours, reactions and responses may not be in alignment with who we are and the soul path we'd like to walk. Then we find books, guides, people, systems or modalities that will help us find our 'right' path, unlearn our old behaviours, and relearn better ways of being. This unlearning and relearning continues ad infinitum if we choose to allow it.

The difference between our internal belief systems and self-sabotaging behaviours is significant.

Self-sabotaging behaviours can be likened to stubbing your toe on the corner of the couch or tripping over your own feet on a flat floor. Often we know that we are the cause of such an action, but instinctively look around to find something to blame - *'Fucking couch, who put that there?'*

Belief systems are much more deeply ingrained in our psyche and subconscious. They are the platform on which we create our life and experience. The lenses we look through to decide how to respond in the world, how to react in certain situations, and how to build and create our lives. These come in through everything we come into contact with - our family of origin, societal expectations, religious persuasions and teachings, schooling, friends, workmates, peers, and so on. Our brains constantly file things away and decide what suits us, what labels we'll own and live to, which ones we'll reject, and how we 'should' live our life.

The journey that begins once we start sifting through the underlying subconscious muck is fascinating, hard, magical, hard, worthy, growth-inducing, and incredibly valuable.

Did I mention it can be really hard?

Creating Golden Opportunity from Leaden Experience

Alchemy = All Chemistry

Alchemy is the ability to transmute, transform and transcend states of being. It is taking the lead of our experience and transmuting it into golden opportunity and new manifestations of wonder and awe within our lives.

When we use Alchemy in our lives, we change the chemical composition of our bodies to increase our ability to simultaneously let light in and out of our being. As we release layers of trauma, stress and conditioning that have dimmed our natural, Goddess-given light, and bring our rejected parts of Self into the fold with love and compassion, we alter our cellular functioning.

I love that doing the internal work has a physiological effect on our physical body, changing neural structures in the brain and chemical compositions at a cellular level. This kind of chemistry transforms me into a science geek! It is science I can get behind. And it's wonderful that more and more scientists are measuring the effects of meditation, somatic therapies and other holistic remedies on brain waves, bodily functioning and creating vitality.

Quantum physicists have proven that the Universe is only 4% physical matter.[1] Therefore, when we look at the physical 'meat suit', the body that houses our soul, it is only 4% of the total picture. The remaining 96% is other elements of our Self, including but not limited to:

Emotional	Mental	Spiritual
Energetic	Relational	Financial
Transformational	Chemical	Hormonal
Metaphysical	Nutritional	Pathological
Psychological	Social	Educational
Organisational	Professional	And so on…
Environmental	Therapeutic	

Everything that happens in any of those areas of our life both affect and effect the coherent functioning of our bodies, the vitality we feel, and the connection to Self and others that we experience.

Most therapies and traditional Western (allopathic) medicine focus on our physical body as a machine and our symptoms are viewed as issues that the machine experiences. As such, they look at replacing parts or inputting chemicals to reduce symptoms, rather than searching for and correcting the root cause. While there is a definite need for that type of medicine in the world, we also must look deep beneath the surface to find root causes and improve our vibrational and ascension frequencies.

---

1   https://www.space.com/11642-dark-matter-dark-energy-4-percent-universe-panek.html

All illness is a message from our spirit to let us know something isn't quite right.

Kinesiology and other somatic body-based therapies look at the feedback loops that are often misaligned or maladapted due to chemical, emotional and physical stress. When we delve into the faulty feedback loops to look for patterns, reprogram the stressors and correct the imbalances with tools, techniques and vibrational remedies, we deal with root causes and start the true process of deep, layered healing.

This is Alchemy at its absolute best!

We reprogram the underlying patterns of emotional, physical or chemical stressors to create realignment and enhance the vibrational signal within our cellular composition.

Awareness of underlying root causes feeding into physical symptomatology empowers healing. Making light where there once was dark, creating space and expansion in place of contraction and blockages. Turning leaden human experience into golden opportunities. Through this work, we regain connection with our Spirit and access to our True God-given Self.

The Truth has 144 Sides

In her book Tuning the Human Biofield: Healing with Vibrational Sound Therapy, *Eileen McKusick recalls Dr Johan Boswinkel saying:*

The truth has 144 sides.

    This instantly resonated in my heart and soul as being SUPER important. This statement packed so much into five little words. I felt like a bomb dropped as so many pieces of multiple life experiences connected. Such a massive 'A-Ha!' moment for me.

    If we take it at face value, this statement merely suggests that our version of the truth is only one small sliver of the actual truth.

    Every single person has varied life experience. We all look at life through different perceptive lenses defined by our experience, subconscious belief patterns, inner talk, culture, the society in which we were raised, and multiple factors besides.

    If we come from the angle that the subconscious mind gives us approximately 400 billion bits of information every second, it makes sense that these numerous filters influence every area of our life, every second of every day. Of this enormous amount of information coming in, we are only consciously aware of around 2000 bits of data[2]. I can't wrap my brain around those exhaustingly massive numbers!

No wonder the truth has 144 sides! Suddenly, I could clearly see so many arguments, differences of opinion, and perspectives on life where I could apply this statement and see the truth from multiple sides. Often our need to be right and win conflicts happens when we try to prove that our filters are the correct and only filters through which people should see the world. It also stems from being shamed, chastised or teased for getting things wrong in the past. We are taught that there is only right and wrong; there is nothing in between. Being wrong comes with hard consequences, so we had better be right, and fight for our rightness.

Here's another way to think about multiple truths. When we perceive what others are thinking about us, what we actually do is project our life filters, upbringing, and subconscious programming into the other person, and then look back at ourselves from their 'perspective' but through our life lenses. We assume that they are thinking what we think in the depths of ourselves about us. We are perceiving their perception of us.

As individuals, we constantly subconsciously worry about our acceptance and belonging in the tribe and, therefore, about what others think of us. As such, the person whose perceptions of judgement we are worrying about is probably standing there concerned with similar

---

[2] *What the Bleep do we Know!?* (Lord of the Wind Film, 2004)

thoughts - and perceiving our perceptions of them.

Can you see how messy this whole truth thing can be? How far from The Truth do you think we are when we are stuck in other people's perceptions of ourselves?

Perhaps this statement of the truth having 144 sides shows us an inbetween position where A + B doesn't always equal C.

What if every single person who sees an issue with different lenses created from their life experiences, belief systems and subconscious programming perceives a different truth than others in the same situation?

Same situation, different perspective, different angle, different conclusion.

This doesn't mean anyone is more right or more wrong. Their perceptions differ based on their life experiences.

For a while I worked with the '360 degrees of truth' theory. When we look at the truth from a 360 degree perspective, we gain a greater awareness from a multitude of angles, but I found that when I used this theory, I put myself in the middle and created the 360 degrees around my own centrepoint. While it did help expand my awareness of other truths, it still felt Self-centric.

'The truth has 144 sides' gave me a more relevant reference point and a refined sense of clarity.

Seeing the truth with 144 sides put an actual human being (who wasn't me) in each of those 144 places, like characters in a movie, or witnesses at a crime scene. I understood that they each have different life lenses, perspectives and more to add to their truth. It took me off centre stage and allowed others a chance to enter.

Everyone has experienced:
- A day when a lack of sleep makes everything grate on your nerves
- A time when the stress is piled so high that another thing could be 'the straw that breaks the camel's back'
- Previous suppression of so much pain, trauma and hurt that emotional responses come out like a Vesuvial volcanic eruption.

During times such as these, our tolerance levels are not what they are when we are well-rested, calm and grounded. They also add to our current experienced truth and the filters through which we look at an event. If we understand that our truth is only one small piece of the truth, we can enter the situation with increased love and compassion, and less judgement and ridicule.

If we take the time to imagine the possibility of other points of view on the 'truth', using our creativity and imagination, then we can gain greater understanding of ourselves and those around us.

We may open to the possibility of choosing to see others with greater respect for the perspective they see as their truth.
We could become less likely to fight others to try and make them see the world from our truth.
We can choose to turn away from shame and blame, and towards acceptance and non-judgement.

Take care to honour the fact that every time we remember an event we have experienced, we only access a memory chain of the original event. Therefore, we remember a time-altered memory rather than the event itself. Even though it may feel significant and real, and the emotions may be visceral in our bodies, we actually only access a memory of our truth. It is still our truth and, as such, we must honour it. But with time, the memory chain of the event lengthens and creates more distance and links from that event to the present incarnation.

Always remember that your truth is your truth and it matters. It matters more than anything else because it is important to you - your health, your wholing, your Spirit, your everything.

Our truth is vitally important to our well-being; acknowledging our truth is often the first (few) stages of healing and reclaiming our sense of Self after trauma, misdirection or change.

In essence, while I have my truth on what happened to me, others will have different truths of who I was, who I am from their own point of truth, their memory of the situations and stories within this book, and about every interaction I've engaged in during my entire life. I hope many remember me well. But I am sure that, because I am messily human, many may not remember me in good light, and others will not remember me at all.

This book contains stories from my truth. I understand that people from my past will have different truths about what happened and I respect their truth. I am also not denying their perspectives of their truth.

I am honouring mine. I choose to honour my experiences with love, compassion, acceptance and honesty. I give you permission, should you be unable to grant it for yourself, to do the same and honour your truth, your experience and your story.

Negative Thoughts and our Propensity for Darkness

Our subconscious programming runs the show approximately 95% of the time. We don't need to think about breathing, minute movements, digestion, immune function, our heart beating and all the naturally occurring bodily functions and systems that keep us alive and moving. This part of our programming is wonderful.

But it starts to become less beneficial when the thoughts in our heads turn over and over. Did you know that a vast majority of these worries never actually come true? And the small percentage of those that do materialise are rarely as bad as we've imagined. In fact, most of the time, we handle things better than we thought we could, and we usually find there is a lesson to learn. Almost all the things we worry about, and ruminate on, are little more than stories the mind creates for entertainment purposes, which we then exaggerate and colour with our belief systems and lenses through which we look at ourselves and life.

Think of how much energy this takes up, and wastes, when it could be used elsewhere.

The good news is that our brains do not distinguish between fact and fiction. They respond to the messages they hear either from external or internal voices. This is why we need to raise our consciousness to become aware of what our internal voice is saying and where we are sending our energy. **Thought energy lasts once we put it out into the world.**

It's amazing the difference we create in our lives when we become consciously aware of our thoughts and work to keep them as positive as possible. But negative thoughts do creep through because of our human conditioning. I love the saying:

Thought energy lasts, it keeps going until it circumnavigates the world and bites us on the arse.

Become aware of the *'What ifs?'* within you. Oftentimes both the positive and negative *'What if?'* will cause stress at the same time. This could be something like: *'What if I get the job? What if I don't?' 'What if they ask for the second date? What if they don't?'*

Because of thought patterns created by ruminating, stress and worry, we often turn both a positive and a negative into something to worry about. We can literally *'What if'* ourselves into an early grave!

Sleepwalking through Life

You may have heard talk about people being *'awake'* and *'asleep'*. I don't particularly like that language because we all have moments of lucidity and other times when we operate on autopilot. It's part of being human.

What people mean by *'awake'* versus *'asleep'* is how aware we are of the subconscious programming that runs our life.

Imagine you're driving to work. You don't need to think about unlocking the car, opening the door, turning your butt, bending your knees to lower yourself into the seat, or swinging your legs into the footwell. Subconscious programming takes care of it for us, and thank goodness for that or we would need a nap within an hour of waking. But it's scary to arrive at work with that thought of *'Shit! How did I get here?'*

We've all experienced time disappearing while we are lost in our subconscious. This is us *'sleepwalking'* through life. In my previous incarnation, before my spiritual awakening, I spent most days living in the future or being stuck in the past. But the only moment is the one we are in right now. Even as you read this, these words fade to become memories to recall at a later date.

The only 'real' time is this second, right now.

Like everything, this can work for and against us. When we use our subconscious to do the menial tasks and keep us alive, we're winning. When we use the natural functioning of our body to devote our time to ruminate, stress and worry, perhaps we're not utilising the power for good but, instead, allowing it to run away with us.

Those who aim for *'awakeness'* simply practise being present as much as possible. When they notice their daydream-like state, they bring themselves back to presence. In the present moment, there is rarely anything life threatening and stress inducing - most of that happens in our mind.

The more we notice our inner thoughts and repetitive patterns, the more we catch ourselves when we drift off.

As a side note, it's important to recognise that daydreaming can be an incredible way to open your imagination, embody your creativity and launch you into wonder. Children daydream all the time and understand the magic of it. As adults, we dismiss its importance as child's play, but we also need that part of us alive, awake, and well.

When we drift off into worry, it is a different picture. Whether a sabre-toothed tiger is actually chasing us, or we have stressful thoughts, the effect on our body physiology is the same. An increase in stress hormones floods our body and, when that happens long term, we end up with health complications and cortisol overloads that can literally take years off our lives. Keep in mind that reducing worry and remaining present when and where you can serves to increase your lifespan - what a huge power to own!

Our brains remember the last thing we say and they cannot distinguish between a positively worded and negatively worded phrase. That's why, when marketing people spruik *'Don't miss out'* people only remember *'Miss out'*. It's more effective to phrase it as *'Book Now'*. Similarly, when we tell ourselves *'I don't need to worry about that'*, our brains hear *'Worry about that'*.

As we become proficient in listening to what we're saying to ourselves, we can work to change the phrases. *'That's too difficult'* could become *'That's less than easy'*. *'I hate (that)'* becomes *'I prefer (this)'*.

This process takes constant vigilance as negativity has the propensity to take over, indulge in the drama, and milk opportunities to stress and worry you. But the mind is like a toddler - don't reason with it, distract it. Give it something shiny and fun to look at, bring in your curiosity and play, and have a laugh with it. Its main job is to keep you safe but, just as you may not trust a toddler to keep you safe, watch what power you are giving your brain.

Your body and the feelings within it are the real signposts. They are the true indicators of where you are and where you need to be. Learn to love, trust and follow them. You'll be amazed at the magic that comes forth.

Journal Prompts

When trying to become more aware of and change our inner voice, we need to have simple, yet effective *'To Do'* steps. Our actions back up our intentions of creating something different in our life:

Listen to your internal critic as you reframe negative into positive.

What are they saying to you in response to that inner thought change?

When you reframe to the positive, what are their objections?

Do you know where these comments have come from? Is there an influential person in your past who limited your potential with their criticism?

Listen for the tone of voice. Watch the body language. How are they standing or acting as they give you this feedback?

What do they want you to do or think instead?

Why do you think they are limiting your creative genius? What are their fears? What's their conditioning?

What would love do instead? How would love respond in this situation?

What is your heart and soul telling you?

What could you say to your internal critic to acknowledge their fears without buying into them?

Ask yourself *'Whose life is it anyway?'*

The Power of Language within Healing

In the beginning was the Word, and the Word was with God, and the Word was God - John 1:1

In the world over, there are many religious references about the power of the spoken word, the language we speak, and sounds we intone. Sound is the highest vibration we can access, and it has powerful healing properties when used well and with knowing.

The language we use, and intention behind the words we choose, is vital to our health and healing. Our *wants* regularly get disguised and framed within us as *don't wants*. Our words carry literal as well as figurative weight, and what we think influences our energy and what we attract into our lives. We can use our language to enhance and give power to our Life Force and energy, or it can be a drain that acts like ballast, keeping us sluggishly stuck and in a state of stress.

Words are powerful. Their intonation, surrounding energy, and expression creates our intention - which is what the Universe acts on when working out the true energy of what we do or don't want to bring into our manifest reality. The development of discernment, awareness and presence is vital for the spells we intone and subsequent containers we create.

A spell is something said three times with intent. For example, if I repeat over and over that *'I am stupid'*, then things will keep coming into my awareness to continually reinforce that belief pattern (our RAS at work again).

'I am' has the same vibrational frequency of the word 'God' and the sound of the Universe, 'Om'. The power of sound and our creation of words is highly significant. It influences our reality. Emotional fluency - the changing of *'I am'* to *'I feel'* with our emotions - becomes a wonderful practice. You will notice that what comes into your life changes as you alter the language you put around it.

To maintain inner truth, alignment and forward motion towards our inner greatness, it's important to watch what we couple with powerful *'I am'* statements.

Our psyche's natural bent for negativity can only be changed with conscious awareness, discernment and choice. Without engaging conscious free-will choice, nothing changes.

When we are fully embodied, we feel the effect language has on our body. It will feel aligned or misaligned with your truth; it will feel heavy and repelling, or lighter and attractive. When we recognise this, we can start to use our body as the indicator of where we need to head in our life, and the choices we need to make.

Our bodies and emotions are the best and most accurate guideposts we have with direct connection to super conscious awareness and our Highest Good.

Letting Go

Imagine holding something precious in your hand, something that makes you who you are - good, bad, ugly or indifferent, it doesn't actually matter. Imagine you've held it tightly, grasped onto it for dear life. That thing controls your thoughts, energy and focus. Holding onto it is tiring.

Do you keep it or let it go?

Now imagine you're standing at the edge of a steep, high cliff. Hold that hand out in front of you, hold it for as long as you can. Draw your focus to your aching arm muscles. Feel yourself tire. Imagine you've held it as part of you forever. Then, let it go. Drop it, let it fall, be rid of it.

That feels like a lot to cope with. The part you've held on to will have given lessons, learnings, experiences, texture or depth to your life, and you've dumped it off a cliff, never to be seen again?

Now, imagine relaxing your grip, bringing your arm to rest gently by your side. You still hold the object, but you can choose when to look at it, how much energy it takes, and whether you need to look at it at all. You are in a gentle space where you can now view it lovingly. You can remember the situation, lessons, learning and experience without the 'thing' controlling you. Now, you can draw strength and the ability to use this part of you as you see fit when other lessons come your way.

I term this concept 'releasing' rather than 'letting go'.

Everything we experience in life adds to our internal tapestry. Completely letting go creates holes - and what do we fill those holes with? If we're conscious, maybe the replacement will be positive, but if we are letting go and leaving a gap there, who's to know what story will grow to fill its space.

Surrender is a similar concept to letting go.

Surrender allows the Divine to hold you, and enables you to hand over control to something greater than yourself. Surrender is accepting things as they are, not creating attachment to what you want them to be, or think they should be. It's very different to giving up.

Oftentimes, when surrender is discussed, the feeling behind it is the energetic frequency of giving up. Feel into your energy and say the following statement knowing that you are supported by the Divine,

I surrendered that to the Universe.

Now, repeat it with the energy of giving up. Can you see how altering your intention changes the way it feels in your body?

When you say it knowing you have Divine support, there is a lightness, faith and connection. You know it is being looked after and that you are cared for.

When we say it with 'giving up' energy, there's a negative vibe and lack of trust, a pretence of faith and no connection to something greater.

The key is discerning the difference in energy when you work in the spiritual realm.

The Words you Use

'Try, might, ought, should, could, maybe, can't' - these words, and more, are powerful and do create limitations.

If we *'should'* have done something, we would have done it. A *'should'* only adds pressure and makes us feel inadequate, as though we're underachieving. When we reframe into a more powerful thought, we move from *'I should have done that'* to *'I chose, or prioritised, to do other things instead'*.

To use a mundane, yet relatable, example, I find shopping around for insurance more than a little bit boring. I get the reminder notice and think *'I should really get onto that'*, then I get the next reminder, and the thought repeats. At this point, I have no intention of actioning anything, but the *'shoulds'* are there.

Then the money exits my account. As soon as I notice, I shop around online and either cancel the policy I've just paid for and organise insurance with another company, or keep the policy where it is, content in the knowledge that I've got the best deal. This exercise is completed and ticked off my 'To Do' list within a couple of hours.

When it needed to get done, it got done. It forced itself to the top of the priority list and was actioned when it needed to be.

How many things in your life are like this? When you *'should'*, you create stress and negative connotations about yourself until the action becomes necessary and gets done.

Be highly aware of using absolutes in language. Words such as *'always, never, everywhere, nowhere, nobody,* *everybody'* paint us into a corner with no room for movement.

'Nobody ever helps me!' Is that true? Nobody? *Ever? 'The kids leave their stuff everywhere around the house!'* Really? In the toilet? On the stovetop? Hanging from the lights?

These may feel like they are true, but absolutes rarely are. In the same way that the truth has 144 sides, there are multiple sides when it comes to how we describe what's going on in our life. The more we work in absolutes, the less room there is for anything else; we are too full with negative assumptions to allow possibility to enter.

In addition, if we are working on the premise that, for example, *'Nobody helps me!'* Guess what? We're going to activate our RAS and welcome in more and more opportunities to prove that this statement is true and real.

Humans do love exaggeration but language carries power and can divide relationships. If you are the one *'always'* doing something, then without even needing to question it, the other *has* to be in the place of the *'never'*.

In relationships, we notice even more subtlety when our language turns towards the negative.

Many people value the importance of a healthy, committed relationship. I'd like you to feel into the word *'devoted'* as opposed to *'committed'*. To me, *'committed'* feels like it has obligation attached to it. It feels responsible, institutionalised, and lacks in wonder, magic and Divinity.

'Devoted' relationships speak of love, respect, deep connection and reciprocity (responding to a positive action with another positive action). The choice of *'devotion'* in relationships, has a much higher ascension frequency than that of *'committed'*. I'm not saying either are right or wrong, but the more we consciously raise

the language we use to speak, think and communicate in this world, and with our spiritual guides and team, the more vibrationally aligned we will be with our Highest Purpose.

Affirmations

Most people on the spiritual path have some form of affirmation that they repeat, have on screensaver, or meditate on. It is important to feel into the energetics around our choice of affirmations before bringing them into our practice.

As with all of our chosen language, *'don't wants'* can be reinforced in our subconscious through our choice of affirmations. We can end up reinforcing what we are trying to release rather than moving toward what we want to bring in. If we choose affirmations that are too far out of reach and contain concepts that are unbelievable to us, we actually program the opposite into our consciousness and reinforce the already existing belief patterns. Beliefs without evidence are delusions, so our affirmations need internal evidence to back up their possibility of truth and manifest them into reality.

If you choose an affirmation like *'I am perfect health'*, yet you suffer with chronic pain, illness and dis-ease, your subconscious mind will be in the background saying something to the effect of *'No you're fucking not!'*

Our bodies recognise misalignments when we choose to recite affirmations that are untrue and we will, in reality, reinforce the opposite statement. Affirmations must feel true; there needs to be possibility, realism, and your internal truth contained in the words, even if they are a stretch from where you are currently.

If, instead, you say *'I choose nurturing and nourishing foods and activities for my body'* that has the possibility of being, or becoming, true even if it is not quite the case yet. Not all our choices are completely healthy, nor are they completely unhealthy. But our affirmations will gradually make changes within our life. You can hold your choice up to the affirmation and ask yourself, *'Is this nourishing and nurturing for me?'*

The more aware you become, the more your choices fall into alignment, and the more positive power your affirmation will contain.

Finally, some words of warning need to be shared in regard to gratitude and affirmations in spiritual practice. In general, gratitude practices and affirmations are wonderful additions to your spiritual repertoire, but you need to be careful with them and choose wisely what you use to programme your subconscious mind.

Even gratitude practices can have negative connotations, energetic imprint and *'don't wants'* masquerading as wants, so clear your energy and tune in carefully as you choose the words you want to use and reinforce.

One of my clients had a fabulous example of this. They had a mantra of *'I have what I need and I need what I have'*. Previously they had been wasteful with their money, buying things that weren't needed but temporarily made them feel good. Whilst this affirmation curbed their spending, it also limited them when welcoming in new levels of wealth and abundance as they didn't *need* anything more than they had. They were firmly anchored to the reality that they had all they wanted and needed in life and that was that.

To upgrade their vibration, and allow them to move to a higher frequency, we reprogrammed this belief system and they hit a 7 figure sales target which had been a pipe dream only months earlier.

Being grateful for what you have is fabulous and necessary, but choose your wording carefully so that you don't limit yourself to old frequencies.

Baby Steps

I am a paradox - as are you. Perfectly imperfect, messily human, divinely guided.

None of these descriptors are either/or, they are both/and. Multiple identifiers are simultaneously true at the same time. None are more right or more wrong; none are better or worse. They all exist in the messy worlds within us.

In my Highest, most Divine Self, I am the creator of my destiny. I am wholehearted, accepting, unconditionally loving and connected to everything and everyone through God Source Oneness. I am brilliantly pure. I am a God-damn Alchemist creating golden opportunities from leaden and messy human experiences.

In my humanness, I am messy - really fucking messy. I am emotional and reactive, I swear and cuss. Highly sensitive, I use defence mechanisms and pain behaviours to force my way through tough situations, while sitting in judgement of myself, and others, as we all try to navigate this messy, yet magnificent, life. Although

I try not to offend or upset others, I know that I have done so, and will do so again.

I am in the arena, getting down and dirty with life, yet showing up the best way I know how and hoping to make a difference.

When life feels like it's railing against me, when things feel unfair and unbalanced, I dive into the shadows and swim in the muck. Hell, at times I roll around and revel in it.

The shadows appear when it feels like everyone else has the upper hand and I feel unheard, unseen, disrespected and unloved. The darkness comes when those from whom I want to receive love respond with judgement, shame and belittling. It also hits hard when those people, for whatever reason, abandon our relationship, sometimes disappearing without explanation, and I am left assuming that I am not a person worth sticking around for.

Throughout my life, I worked hard to maintain my connection to others and fit into their boxes, yet backtracked on my own values and morals to do so. As a result, the path to Self felt concealed and too far to travel, too scary to explore. I didn't recognise who I'd become. I compromised everything that I loved about myself to become acceptable to others and connect with them. They never had a chance to like me, let alone love me.

They didn't know who I was because I was so busy trying to be what I thought they wanted me to be that I wasn't there, wasn't present.

A number of stories propelled me along my current spiritual path. I share these because they broke me out of the cycle of constantly looking outside myself for validation, acceptance and love and, instead, turned me to look at my heart and feel into my soul for the answers that were true for me. They tuned me into guideposts that may have looked crazy to everyone else. But these were my directions back to me, no matter how absurd they looked to people on the outside of my life.

These stories also stayed at the top of my mind, especially in the early days, to guarantee that I didn't turn back to my old life, my old self, even though at times that felt like the easiest, safest and most 'appropriate' thing to do. They were the gateway between illness and wellness, depression and vitality, self-loathing and self-love.

When we empower ourselves through the challenges that come our way, and learn from our past, we become creators of our own destiny. We choose how we proceed, and we have the opportunity to use our experiences to evolve and grow, rather than remain where we are.

From Selfless or Selfish to Self-Full

The first Women's Circle I attended felt 'woo-woo' and out there but, as I'd known the facilitator for a while, I trusted her. I had no idea what it entailed or what we'd do, but felt drawn to go. Super early in my spiritual rekindling, I was nervous about going somewhere without the support of friends, and I was way out of my comfort zone.

Selfless or selfish? During a group discussion, one of the ladies spoke about the difference between selfless and selfish.

'Selflessness' does what it says on the tin. It makes less of yourself. We often give, and give, and give, to the detriment of our own needs and wants, in our efforts to look after others. This over-generosity can lead us into resentment spirals where we truly begrudge what we are giving to others because it feels one-sided and lacks reciprocity.

'*Selfishness*' is doing something for yourself that hurts another, disrespects them or creates disharmony in a relationship.

Then a participant mentioned that she'd learned a word - 'Self-Full'.

Wow! I didn't even know that was a possibility. Filling your own cup or putting on your own oxygen mask BEFORE helping others? I didn't think that was allowed. It certainly wasn't encouraged in the world I lived and within my idea of normal.

I left the circle a different person. On top of my burgeoning inner strength and grace, I had this whole new idea that I could give myself permission to look after me, and not constantly work myself into the ground for other people. I didn't yet know how this new knowledge and support would manifest in my life, but I had discovered a new-found curiosity to ask questions of myself and find out.

Self-Full was definitely something I needed to explore.

Years later, a YouTube clip from spiritual channel Esther Hicks, caught my attention. She said:

There is no such thing as selfishness.

Think about it! Every time you've been called '*selfish*' by someone, it's usually because they want something from you that you are unwilling to give.

That really resonated, not only because people have called me selfish, but because I have also done the same to others. The selfish person is actually the one asking something of the other, when they have no capacity or desire to give it to them.

After that realisation, *'selfish'* was left out of the equation. My awareness shifted to *'selflessness'* and *'Self-Fullness'*. Even now, I can slip into old habits of doing too much for others without nourishing myself adequately, falling into exhaustion and resentment. In that space, nobody benefits. Recognition of this tendency helps me consciously shift into giving nourishment to myself, allowing myself to receive nurturing and moving into Self-Fullness.

When giving to others from a *'Self-Full'* place, we are much more effective in our lives and can be *'of service'* to others as equals, rather than act like we are inferior and *'in service'* to them.

You are not Broken

Desperate for help early in my healing journey, I attended my first Kinesiology session with no idea what to expect. I'd been unwell for what felt like years; I was teary all the time; I felt like a broken shell of a human being and life itself felt almost impossible. Filled with self-hatred, my relationship had been toxic for years, and I felt unseen, unheard, unloved, unworthy, and a million other things besides. None of my feelings were particularly positive.

Sitting with the practitioner, I blurted out:

> *I'm broken. I need to fix myself enough to save my relationships. They're falling apart and it's all my fault.*

That session changed my life. At one point, the practitioner said:

I don't think you understand how emotionally abused you are, and have been.

Everything clicked. A number of my major relationships sprang immediately to mind, and I realised that I needed to change, learn more about what I wanted for me, and create loving boundaries for myself that would keep me safe.

I walked out of there feeling less desolate and as though there might actually be light at the end of the deep, dark tunnel I was stuck in.

It took four months for the deepest of those emotionally and psychologically abusive relationships to become clear. But, once the light shone on my experiences, my personal growth took off. As I broke free from underlying patterns, I gave myself space to heal, to learn who I was, and to connect deeper to the spirituality I had long abandoned.

For at least the next 12-18 months I thought back to *'when I was broken'* and referenced that in my healing:

'I was broken back then'
'I've done so much work, I'm glad I'm not as broken now'
'I was a broken shell of a human'

A million versions of that comment came out of my mouth and ran through my head. Then, one brave soul gave me a dressing down:

You were never broken. You were a lot of things, but you weren't broken. That implies there was something fundamentally wrong with you and that you were faulty. God doesn't make no junk.

As mere mortals, who are we to judge, shame and belittle the creations of the Divine Creator of the Universe?

We do not have overarching sight over the intricacies of the Universe. And who are we to deny and rubbish our existence and hate ourselves to such an extent?

We all have a purpose. We are all vitally needed. We are all threads in a global tapestry, perfectly placed to play our part, and, when removed, we create a hole, gap and loss for those around us.

As much as I was a fan of self-flagellation and mental torture, I agreed with her words. Brokenness wasn't part of the picture.

'Messily human?' Yes, I could own that.

Don't let that C**t Steal your Bricks

I'd love to tell you that my story is unique. In one way it is because it happened to me, with me, and for me. But, I've heard versions of everything I have experienced within other people's lives. Heartache, pain, deep trauma, consuming grief, abuse, terror - the whole spectrum. Part of the mess of human experience, life occurs on a spectrum of amazing to terrible, wonderful to shitty. And through these experiences, we are given incredible stories of resilience, overcoming challenges, and becoming the phoenix rising out of the ashes.

Let me get this clear - I used to hate the word 'cunt'. I found it crass, vulgar and offensive.

One night, a friend of mine came over for wine. Although we didn't really know each other well at the time, we clicked immediately and spoke about everything that night. Our relationships, our traumas, and our wins….it was truly magical. There were tears, laughter, and a conversation about the 'C-word'.

They told me that I shouldn't be offended by the word as I owned one, and that I could only be offended by it if I chose to be. It was the use of it by those that didn't have one, and who threw it at women as an insult, that was offensive, not the word itself. They had been to see the play *The Vagina Monologues*; as part of the show, the audience had to do an exercise where they shouted 'cunt' at the top of their lungs over and over again, until they were all comfortable with reclaiming and owning the word.

That night in my living room, they got me to do the same. I remember the two of us repeatedly shouting together, until we collapsed in fits of laughter.

That scene still plays fondly in my mind - I smile when I think of it. It was much more empowering than I ever thought it could be. And, I haven't had a problem with the word since. Amazing how it worked!

So, how does that relate to stopping the cunts from stealing your bricks?

A local friend invited me to attend my second Women's Circle. Although it still felt a little mystical and out there, not to mention well beyond my comfort zone, it also felt exactly what I needed.

I was in the process of ending an extremely toxic relationship that was full of abuse from both of us - we fought fire with fire and the inferno had been out of control for a very long time. It was hard, horrible and the main contributor to the chronic fatigue and autoimmune picture of my health. My physical body was crumbling under the weight, and my emotional and mental selves were unhealthy and spent. I had nothing left and couldn't remember the last time I'd felt any happiness, connection or love.

At the time, I was willing to try anything that may help me along this new path I'd decided to walk. Since I'd made the decision to leave this particular relationship, a little ignition light burned deep in my gut and I was curious about what this signified. I wanted to see how I could nourish and nurture the flame. A long, lost piece of me, sitting deeper in my soul than I'd bothered looking since I hit puberty, was starting to make itself known, and I was both excited and curious at its presence.

Before I left for the Women's Circle, I made sure my home was organised within an inch of its life. Everything was done to try and avoid another outburst prior to going out but, as I was getting ready, yet another toxic and pointless argument broke out between my partner and me. When I took the bins out for collection, they followed me out, furiously continuing the argument with venom in their voice, eyes and energy field.

As I started to walk back towards the house, they tried to intimidate me. They walked towards me, stood closer than was comfortable, made themselves bigger and more threatening, and frightened the hell out of me. I thought they were going to hit me, or worse, so I pushed them.

They turned on their heel and sneered over their shoulder as they headed back towards the house,

You just touched me! That's assault. I'm ringing the police and reporting you.

In my mind, I was protecting myself and hadn't done anything wrong but, after multiple threats from them, terror took over. I ran inside, grabbed my bag and phone, and flew out of the house. Running to my friend's, I called a lawyer who told me to immediately head to the police station, make a report and get an interim intervention order (IVO).

Sobbing and shaking like a leaf, I arrived at my friend's house, and relayed the story to them before asking them to drive me to the police station on the way to the Circle.

At the station, the constable asked me the details of what happened prior to and during the event, as well as a bit about our relationship. It was truly the first time anyone had labelled what I was going through as Domestic Violence. The police officer told me I needed to apply for an IVO but something internal stopped me following that advice. I didn't feel like I could do that to them. While they were extremely toxic with me, I was concerned that taking that action would inflame things further - and I also wasn't used to thinking about protecting myself from harm.

Over the following years, I occasionally wished that I made a different choice, but I also know that I've grown more as a result of making the choice I did. *(Please note: This is not the right choice for everybody and please trust your instincts and advice. These measures are there to help protect you from abusers and are vital for your safety if needed.)*

From there, my friend drove us to the Women's Circle.

Visibly shaking, I was very teary. Luckily, it was a safe space to experience all the emotions flowing through me. As we went around the circle, I listened to other women introduce themselves and share their stories. I actually can't remember if I passed my speaking turn to the next woman or choked out some words through my tears.

Then, the woman leading the Circle led us into a guided meditation where we were to meet our *'Inner Wise Person'*. Losing myself in my subconscious mind was lovely. It felt as though time stopped as I was led through the usual meditation scenario.

She guided us into a lush garden surrounding a calm oasis. A sanctuary, a safe space amongst a circle of plants. I lay down on a soft, round padded bed in the middle of a ring of flowers, and curled into the foetal position. As my inner wise person was called into the scene, they wrapped themselves around me, encircling my physical body with a calm and knowing presence. I felt safe, protected and held.

Guided to get a message from them, I tuned into my guide and heard:

'You've made great headway, you're building solid foundations on which you can soon start building your fantastic new life. You're almost ready to start building up,

just don't let that cunt steal your bricks.'

Well, it took all my energy not to burst out in laughter. All I could think was, *'Yep, that's something my inner wise person would say.'* It felt great to laugh and release some of my pent-up tension and stress.

I don't believe this message from my Inner Wise Person was directed towards a single individual, despite the situation it followed. It was a wider warning to me that I'd been *'giving away my bricks'* to others all my life, prioritising others' needs above my own and depreciating my own value. This was a call to change, a time for me to prioritise myself and rise from the ashes of my previous way of being, to become more true and whole. To solidify my foundations, I needed to hold on to my own bricks and, when ready, build a new life supported by my lessons of the past.

We all have C**ts who try to Diminish us

It doesn't matter what their motivations are. Sometimes people believe that they are expressing love or protecting us. At other times, they want what they perceive is best for us as though they, not us, understand our inner desires. Alternatively, some people deliberately trip us up, or piss on our fire to extinguish our flames.

> *It is our perception of what's going on that matters.*
> *It's how we store it in the body, how we process it.*

One person's trauma can be another person's fuel. It all depends on our reaction, personality, perception, and remembrance of what happened at the time.

The 'cunt' could be anyone: an ex or current partner, a parent, sibling, family member, grandparent, teacher, colleague, religious leader, friend, anybody you come in contact with. They could be a person you've only run into once or twice, but they rent room in your head as you keep replaying the diminishing incident. Some of the cunts are people we deeply love, who are unaware of their negative effect on our life. When those you love steal your bricks, they aren't always filled with the intent to make you miserable but it is, however, a side effect of their actions and words.

This feeling of being diminished can grow through regular abuse or bullying, but sometimes it is through repeated comments about your physical attributes, intelligence, spiritual ideations or any number of things you hold dear. It could be that you don't feel seen, heard or understood by loved ones, or you feel invisible, unworthy, unloved or disrespected, or that you don't belong.

So, how do we build resilience against those who steal our bricks when we try to rebuild our lives, or build a new aspect to our existing life?

We build our internal resilience, heal our traumas, construct solid emotional and energetic foundations, and develop strong spiritual practices.

When Friends Speak Up

I am blessed to know a dear friend who shares my whacky sense of humour, and is direct, funny and uplifting. One day, they turned to me and said, straight out:

> *I don't think you understand how fucked up your relationships are.*

I looked at them with disbelief and confusion:

> *I don't understand. What do you mean? Isn't all this normal?*

They shook their head with equal, if not more, disbelief, and explained that relationships are supposed to be fun, reciprocal, give and take, supportive, and that usually you enjoy spending time with your romantic partner. What an alien concept! It had been so long since I'd experienced that feeling.

As we discussed healthy relationships, I was gobsmacked. I truly felt like I'd been blindsided.

My relationship was my normal.
Abusive comments were my normal.
Lack of reciprocity was my normal.

I was blown away. I hadn't understood why people enjoyed being around their intimate partners so much. I certainly didn't look forward to one-on-one time with mine.

Every single day I am grateful for the courage of this person. Without somebody brave enough to call out the lack of normality, explain to me how healthy relationships were supposed to work, and lovingly clarify what thriving connections looked like, I wonder where I'd be today? **During my journey of self-discovery, I have been blessed with the perfectly positioned outspoken people at exactly the right times.**

Sometimes, like on this occasion, I've been left with my jaw hanging open, completely shocked by their bravery in speaking up, surprised by how receptive I've been to welcome their words, and how clear the misbehaviours in both myself and others became visible through the experiences.

To all those people, I thank you. I love you. I am grateful for your input in my life.

Keep being brave, keep speaking up and keep changing the parts of the world that you touch.

External Influence

Throughout our life we have two main choices. Do we listen to the internal voice of our inner knowing or submit to the external voice of our society, tribe and others?

More often than not, due to our physiological desire to remain safe, protected and belong with others in connection and communion, we choose to submit to the external influences. We look to them for validation and the green tick of approval - *'Yes, that's how you're supposed to behave'*.

Dr Brené Brown states in *The Gifts of Imperfection*:

Belonging is the innate human desire to be part of something larger than us. Because this yearning is so primal, we often try to acquire it by fitting in and by seeking approval, which are not only hollow substitutes for belonging, but often barriers to it. Because true belonging only happens when we present our authentic, imperfect selves to the world, our sense of belonging can never be greater than our level of self-acceptance.

Well, fuck me. I'd been getting this wrong most of my life. Submitting myself in servitude to others and what I perceived they wanted me to be, rather than daring to actually show up in the world and my relationships as me. Yet, when I did have the guts to show up as myself, the *right* people came into my life and loved me for me. Problem was, I was trying to fit in with all the people I was *supposed* to be like and perform like.

To explore why we let external influences rule our way of being, let's look at the unfulfilled needs that drive our behaviours. As we overwork, overwhelm and 'busy' ourselves, our drivers tell us a story. An underlying narrative of why we're not good enough just as we are, why we need to work harder than everyone else, and why we are unworthy of the success that others have.

If we learn to spend time in quiet contemplation with those thoughts, emotions and externalised behaviour patterns, we can begin to understand the underlying conditioning, make friends with what lies beneath, and bring it back into the fold of our being with compassion and grace.

Often, the underlying thought patterns that influence our behaviours are obvious, and we don't need to dig too far to find them. But, other times, they are hidden deep in the subconscious, in a place we're unable to find until other layers of healing are peeled back to reveal what lies beneath. However it comes for you, the right layers always appear at the right time for healing and uncovering, for bringing back into the Self and wholing.

One of the obvious sacrifices we make for the external 'greater good' is that we need to forfeit ourselves for the sake of our children.

We put aside our wants, needs, desires and dreams to protect our children. To make sure they have everything they need and prioritise them to the detriment of our own health and vitality. I'd like to say this is a minority of women but, unfortunately from what I've seen, it isn't.

To heal, many women must learn to prioritise themselves. To put themselves first and recognise that they are important too. Without thriving and following our hearts and dreams, we continue to peddle the societal belief that women should be 'paused' while they support the community.

Our children then learn subconsciously from the way we treat ourselves and our demonstrated actions, that women aren't allowed to prioritise themselves and, so, the cycle repeats.

A significantly better lesson for our children is to see their parents and caregivers love themselves fully, wholly and without condition. Imagine seeing your parent take time to 'fill their cup', do what lights them up, and bring their magic into the world. I love to see people live their best lives. It inspires me, makes me believe that anything is possible, and helps with what I can manifest.

Instead of passing on self-sacrifice, self-flagellation and people-pleasing to our children, what if we gave the gift of internal knowingness, self-fullness and self-love?

Many people stay in relationships long past their use-by date 'for the children'. But what do we demonstrate by doing this? Think of your relationship - would you be happy for your children to be in one the same as you are currently experiencing? Would you want them to be loved the way you're being loved?

For those in unhappy or toxic marriages, staying for the children is detrimental to everyone. I learned very early on in healing that:

*What is loving towards yourself is always loving to everyone.
And the converse is true too.
What is detrimental towards yourself is always detrimental to everyone.*

By subscribing to the story that we are doing it for others, we often hold ourselves to things that are not in our Highest Good. If it is detrimental to us, it is *always* detrimental to everyone. When we are not thriving, vital and full of energetic life, we tend to give out of resentment, obligation and because we feel we *have* to.

What are we teaching? What do we want others to learn?

When I was young, there was someone in my life who was highly inappropriate with the affection they showed. Without many tools at my disposal, I chose rudeness as a way of building a wall to keep myself safe. I couldn't mention what was happening because I needed to 'protect' the adult, even though I knew what they were doing was wrong. My parents would have been devastated, and I couldn't bear the thought of upsetting them and creating a rift between them and this other party.

Rather than anyone asking a usually polite, people-pleasing girl why she was rude to this one particular adult, I was regularly told off and ordered to be nicer. The catch phrase *'Where are your manners?'* rang constantly in my ears.

The external influence I listened to was that, as a child, I needed to be polite, kind and submit to my elders regardless of their actions. But my internal self was screaming that it was wrong and I needed to speak up. That splitting of influence and a lack of resources meant that I felt torn in two, at odds with right and wrong, and I ended up owning the blame, shame, disgust and wrongness purely to please others.

When we see behaviours that are out of the ordinary, it may be helpful to look at the potential root cause that may have influenced the person displaying them, rather than dishing out retribution and punishment for those actions. We can come from the angle of empathy, curiosity and non-judgement to ask why their behaviour has changed. By connecting and giving a safe space, we can help others regulate their internal world and learn to trust their inner knowing, rather than the external influences that feel too weighty for young shoulders.

Adults need to learn these skills so that we can pass them on to the next generation and break these ingrained cycles that are so prevalent in society. By listening to our heart, soul and internal compass, we will not become a world of selfish fuckers, but a realm of loving, connected, empathic humans.

Every day gives us lessons in what we do out of obligation, and what we do out of love. Each of these will teach us something that will either move us away from our purpose and goals, or towards the magic we crave.

Every day, these lessons build our internal structure. All we can do is keep learning and building the structure we desire.

The Inner Self versus the Outer Self

Our internal landscape and reality is often heavily impacted by external influences, conditioning and relationships. We think our external world is who we are and what we are about. We base our idea of self on other people's comments, criticisms, feedback and perception of ourselves, and forget to check in with what feels right in our heart and soul. Then we build our life to other people's expectations and specifications trying to be 'good enough', 'loveable enough', and 'responsible enough'.

We are taught to trust the thinking brain as Monarch of our experiences, and to distrust our inner voice, intuition and actual experiences. As such, we look externally for validation, acceptance and connection with others before checking internally to see if that path is best for us, or if we need to head in our own direction.

Do you let other people's opinions get in the way of living your authentic truth?

We forget that our truth doesn't need to make sense to anybody else - it only needs to make sense to us. It needs to feel right in our heart and to resonate in our gut. Oftentimes, we close down and ignore that little voice because we believe it's not what we *should* be doing.

Every time we live to other people's *'shoulds'* we are ignoring our soul a little more. We deny the parts of ourselves that want to come out, express themselves to the world, and emerge from dark and leaden heaviness into the golden light.

Part of our desire to hide our true self is the ancient part of the brain that tells us, *'If you aren't accepted, loved and embraced by your tribe, you'll be kicked into the wilderness to die'*. While that sounds harsh, our brain and thought patterns work in the black and white duality of life/ death, yes/no.

Society at large works to the pendulum of duality - if you're not with us, you're against us; if you're not right in what I sense as right, then you're wrong.

Our perceived idea of safety is, therefore, why we regularly deny parts of ourselves. Fear comes to the fore, telling us that we will be rejected and abandoned for being unloveable, unworthy, and not good enough. We regularly forget that failure and mistakes are a natural part of the path of life, the passage to our perceived success, and the learning we need to embody to make it back to our True Self.

At some point your spirit wants to come out. It wants to see the light of day. To express your true nature, true beauty, divine love, and internal Divinity. Your desire to express the full and True essence of who you are starts to bubble within, looks for an outlet, and speaks to you in louder tones until you begin to listen.

You are here to light up the world.
You are here to excite.
You are here to feel joyful.
You are here to live a wondrous life.

That doesn't mean you will experience a life without pain or challenges! It means that you will live a full, rich, completely expressed and fully-felt life, without denial and suppression of the hard parts.

Think about when you first meet someone. *'What's your name?'* and *'What do you do?'* are usually the first questions asked.

The external idea that *'you are what you do for a living'* shows the extent that we are judged by surface façades. How you dress, who your friends are, your job, the area in which you live - and so many other factors. Yet, when we dip into them, how many of those are actually who we are?

We often define ourselves by the roles we play in life - parent, partner, sibling, friend, child, etc. This isn't always a problem, but it can be when we feel that 'box' is restrictive and opposes our spirit. And, when we come to define ourselves in that role, we reduce who we are to that identifier.

One client, a high-level executive CEO, defined themselves by this measure of success.

When they came to see me, they spoke proudly of their role but, as we dug deeper and went into the underlying, subconscious trauma, they felt that being a CEO didn't allow any room for fun, play and excitement.

Every time they walked into the office to 'keep up the appearance' of what they thought was socially acceptable for a 'CEO' to be, they denied that part of themselves.

They perceived a CEO as someone who is responsible, successful, in charge, and has their shit together all the fucking time.

It was exhausting. Under the heavy cloak of responsibility lay this other aspect of a human who wanted fun, play, lightness and connection *along with* responsibility.

But, once we uncovered their underlying trauma, they were able to realise that the two could exist together. It wasn't an either/or, it was a both/and. When they made and embodied that realisation, it actually gave them a more solid platform for greater abundance, success and connection within the work environment.

Bringing fun and play to work didn't mean that seriousness didn't have a necessary place. But it did give the opportunity for access to increased creativity, and brought an expansion to them which had previously been unexplored due to the constriction of what a CEO was perceived to be in their previous mindset.

What is your Reality?

It is time to switch up our thinking and look internally to explore our reality. Most people have multiple selves. I was no different, with a multitude of selves for work, intimate relationships, immediate and extended family, friends, and everyone besides. Playing all those parts was exhausting.

It felt as though a different hat was required for each occasion. I spent my days trying to read each situation and find a way to fit in. I played a variety of roles and tried on different, *'more palatable'* personalities, purely because I never felt like the True, inner me was acceptable and loveable just as she was.

Although I was included in activities at school, I always felt on the outer, wandering between groups to keep my options open. This was, most likely, a defence mechanism so that nobody would learn the truth of my nature. I deeply believed that I was strange, unloveable, a bit away from centre, and unworthy of deep connection. Sitting on the outside edges of a group, yearning for connection, became my normal existence.

One of my roles was that of the *'best friend'* you hung out with when you fell out with your best friend. Playing that part was my specialty, especially in high school. As such, I learned to control my behaviour, play the *'good girl'*, and work at pleasing everybody. I stuffed my True Self into an inner cupboard, terrified that one day it would burst out and my 'life' would be over, the game would be up.

This behaviour continued into my adult life, where I tried to be who I perceived others wanted me to be. I wanted to please my family, friends, bosses, partners, anyone I came in contact with. The *'rescuer'* and *'pleaser'* were strong in me; eventually they overworked me into chronic illness.

Growing up, I was told that relationships were hard. And, as an overachieving people-pleaser, I figured:

Man, I'm killing it in the relationship game! My relationships are hard as fuck. A+ for me.

When I spoke to someone about a relationship that I regularly struggled with, I repeatedly received this advice:

You can't change others, you can only change yourself and your reactions to the situations.

While that is true within a certain context, it also reinforced my beliefs that I was broken, not good enough and flawed. If the other was as perfect as they always told me they were, then I was wrong because I didn't see their perfection, only their flawed humanness. All this became internalised and backed up my inner dialogue of being unloveable and unworthy.

I believed that I needed to:
- Change to make everyone else happy
- Give up my wants and needs to ensure other people's happiness
- Bend and contort myself into more acceptable and palatable shapes to find love, happiness and acceptance.

If I didn't, then it was all my fault. I was once again the failure; once again not good enough. Everyone else was perfect, and the problem was me.

All I wanted was to be loved and accepted, but how could anyone do that fully when I didn't love myself? I didn't allow anyone in, and I kept my full truth hidden away in shame and embarrassment.

My biggest 'A-Ha' hit when I found the truth that I wasn't broken and didn't need to change myself to save my relationships.

I needed the courage to change to save myself from myself. And, when I did that, the right people entered my life, the right relationships found me without hassle or manipulation. I did not need to contort myself into shapes that weren't natural for me to live in.

It was time to discover what I wanted and needed, to explore what made me happy, to go deep within and reconnect to my heart, soul, spirit and the Universe.

I was so busy looking for acceptance and external validation that it felt like I needed an opinion or answer for everything. Back then, I'd chime in and give an ill-informed opinion, state my case, or jump on a bandwagon so I didn't seem stupid or out of touch. But all my validation-seeking got me was a few strange looks and surface level connections. It was connection through common enemy intimacy, not the real, deep, honest intimacy that I deeply craved.

This is Me

This acceptance of my limitations has reduced the number of selves I need to be so I can feel accepted. I may not show all of my facets to everyone I meet, but the more healing work I have done, the fewer hats I wear and roles I play. It is reduced to a simple *'This is me'*.

Others can take me as I am, or not take me at all. I am not, and will never be, to everyone's taste, and even those I am loved by may not always like me. No longer do I wear façades of pretence to keep people happy. Those who love me for who I am can now clearly see me, be attracted to me, and enter into my life.

What is Trauma?

Traumas do not have to be large, earth shaking and terrifying. Any experience where we feel less than loved, nurtured and nourished can be embodied within us as a traumatic event.

'Trauma' comes from the Greek word meaning 'wounding'. This doesn't mean that every hard, challenging and painful event gets stored as a traumatic wound. If we are able to be supported during the entire stressful event, process it, and come to a resolution, then the event doesn't need to be stored within the body as a memory.

Gabor Maté, a specialist in childhood development and trauma says in the film, *The Wisdom of Trauma*:

Trauma is not what happens to you. Trauma is what happens inside you, as a result of what happens to you.

This explains why something that is traumatic to one person will not be experienced as traumatic to another.

Some traumas are a constant drip rather than a flash flood. Where once you brushed it off, and pretended it didn't mean anything, it then grows harder and harder to remain non-reactive and to leave the comments where they belong. Instead, the actions eventually take hold in your psyche and influence your thoughts, emotions and behaviours. It is like that persistent drip fills your bucket until it spills over and consumes you with trauma.

Trauma has two main stages.

The first stage is when the trauma is new and raw - an open, unhealed wound. When it's new, it's highly sensitive to pain. As long as it remains in this open, raw and unhealed state, the owner of the trauma will experience severe pain and react in an overwrought pattern when it's touched or activated, even lightly.

We eventually grow scar tissue over these open wounds. Scar tissue has no nerve endings, so we don't feel. It's hard, inflexible and incapable of new growth, which restricts our potential for newness and creativity. At this point, we often choose numbing behaviours such as alcohol, drugs, sex, online shopping or binge eating to distract ourselves from our internal landscape and the resolution of our trauma.

With either form of trauma we defend ourselves against the pain through symptoms such as physical illness, addictions and other numbing behaviours, and emotional withdrawal. Our perception is often that it will hurt less to numb our pain than to feel it, yet the behaviours we choose to avoid our pain often kill us slowly in the 'death by paper cut' type of way.

Longer relationships tend to be more triggering or activating because, the longer we are involved in communion with someone, the more stories, ties and chances for misunderstanding, hurt and conflict exist. Oftentimes we want to placate, tend to and protect these relationships due to their longevity. As such, we regularly hide and suppress our True Self because we are unsure whether the other person will like, approve of, and accept us, as we change. When we remove previously prevalent behaviours, we change from their expectations and perceptions of who they think we are.

One client I worked with repeatedly told me that they had no trauma and, therefore, couldn't understand why they were having problems. They loved their parents dearly, and felt loved in return, but they also felt that huge expectations were placed on them, and they were always expected to perform to a high level. As a result, they never felt that they lived up to these lofty goals, and spent their life feeling like they weren't quite hitting the mark in any area of their life, despite trying their best.

This is one of those 'constant drips in the bucket' scenarios. No, the parents weren't abusive, but the client felt the weight of their expectations and the disappointment of not quite living up to their lofty ideals as a trauma within their subconscious mind. In clearing the client's vibrational frequency and upgrading them to a greater sense of self acceptance, love and compassion, knowing they always did and do their best in any situation, the relationship with their parents improved from good to great. What a win! No, their parents didn't intend to hurt them, and they didn't always read it as such, but when the awareness came, it allowed a huge expansion and growth that had been waiting for the right time to bloom in the light of day.

Fight, Flight, Freeze, Fragmentation, Fawn

Most people are aware of the trauma reactions of our nervous system when we are in a stress response - fight, flight and freeze - and in Kinesiology, we take that even further and add fragmentation. Fawning is an additional trauma response within the vagal nerve system

Fight and **Flight** are pretty obvious and well documented. When in an emergency, we either want to fight or run away.

Freeze is where we try to fight and flight at the same time, and end up like a deer in the headlights, unable to move and rendered incapacitated.

Fragmentation, which I've not heard anywhere other than within a Kinesiology setting, is where we either fall to pieces in the moment or have left pieces of ourselves in those traumas of our past. This means that when we are faced with an immediate stressor, we either fall apart or can't respond effectively, simply because we're not all there.

Fawning is the stress response of people pleasing, complying, accommodating others - and is our way of avoiding or further mitigating trauma. This stress response is particularly prevalent in abusive relationships, people suffering from PTSD, and co-dependence.

Each of these stress responses are reactions to ensure we stay alive and out of harm's way. Often, however, we interrupt the stress response so the event gets energetically stuck within the body. Each trauma should have a beginning (where we get the response), a middle (where we have a reaction) and an ending (where the stress is resolved).

Imagine a squirrel in life-threatening danger from a fox. That squirrel falls into a freeze response - playing dead while the fox sniffs it to see if it will be a tasty meal. During the freeze response, the squirrel will not move, slowing its breathing to unnoticeable levels. Once the fox loses interest and moves away, the squirrel jumps up, shakes itself violently, and runs until the adrenaline is no longer coursing through its veins. It allows itself to complete the trauma cycle.

Humans do not allow ourselves to honour this innate process. We suppress the trauma, pull up our bootstraps, take it in our stride, tell ourselves we're overreacting, or any number of other socially acceptable responses. As such, the natural adrenal response gets stuck in our personal reactionary pattern.

Comparative Suffering

Many times during our healing journey we deny our own trauma, refuse to look at it fully and belittle our own experience because we *'don't have it as bad as other people'*. We hold other people's trauma in higher regard than our own, and diminish ourselves because our suffering is inferior - *'At least I don't have cancer'*, *'At least my child's healthy'*, *'At least I have a job'*, *'At least my partner only screams at me and hasn't hit me'*.

If we compare our suffering to another person's, we will always be able to find someone who has it worse off than us.

Dr Brené Brown talks of comparative suffering in her research work on shame, vulnerability and leadership.

She says in her book, *Rising Strong*:

> *Comparative Suffering is a function of fear and scarcity. Falling down, screwing up, and facing hurt often lead to bouts of second guessing our judgement, our self-trust, and even our worthiness. 'I am enough' can slowly turn into 'Am I really enough?' If there's one thing I've learned over the past decade, it's that fear and scarcity immediately trigger comparison, and even pain and hurt are not immune to being ranked.*

When in the state of comparative suffering, we look for those who are better or worse to validate our internal story, experience and beliefs. We rank and compare our suffering.

What can feel even more painful is when people diminish our hurt and pain by telling us that others have it worse. This can often force us further down the comparative suffering path, leading us into shame and guilt for having spoken up about our experiences. It can also mean that we dismiss our day-to-day trials and tribulations because they aren't 'worthy' enough of admitting they are traumatic events for us.

That took me a lot of time to understand. Even when I was well into my healing journey, I'd dismiss my experienced emotional and psychological abuse, immediately going into the state of comparative suffering.

This is damaging, when we hear it from ourselves and from other people in our life.

Moving towards Desire

In your healing and wholing journey, be careful you don't continue to focus on, return to, and reactivate your traumas. If we get stuck in that state of being, we can never move forward to better things because we remain in the past.

As we heal, we also need to address our worthiness, loveability and self-respect, allowing that to move us forward at the same time as healing and disconnecting from the past trauma. It is the difference between changing our vibration to an ascension frequency, rather than consistently reactivating old wounds, taking us back to what impedes us, rather than opening up to the possibilities for the future.

Keep moving towards your desires. Cyndi Dale in *Energetic Boundaries* says:

> *The law of physics is pretty clear. Nature abhors a vacuum, so when something goes out, something else must come in.*

This is vital when we are working through the healing and wholing processes because it helps us remain focussed on where we want to be. As we shift old energetic patterns out of our being, what do we want to replace them with?

Usually something with a greater vibrational frequency that leads us towards ascension and growth rather than contraction and stagnation. This is why it's important to always keep at least one eye on the future while healing the past. We want to move forwards towards our desires.

If we can learn to elevate our own trauma to the level that we hold others' trauma sacred, we are able to move forward in leaps and bounds towards wholing and a return to Self. This doesn't mean that we don't have empathy and compassion for others, it simply means that we practice turning that empathy and compassion towards ourselves as well as others. When we are able to do that, we can hold necessary space for everyone - both ours and their stories are able to be true at the same time:

Yes, they are suffering with that AND I am suffering with this.

Remove the either/or, the yes/but, the excuses, the justifications and the belittlement.

The only way to fully process our trauma and stress responses so that we grow, transform and transmute, is to feel our emotional responses in their full messiness and allow them to move through our systems, get processed and release them to the ether.

Remember that to heal, you need to address within you the lead that holds you down and alchemise it into the golden light of your being so you can walk your path. When you do this, you grant yourself permission to help others in pain because you have walked the path of healing and acceptance without comparison and judgement.

My Best is Good Enough

When life gets on top of us, we can fall deeply into perfectionism. Our desire to control, perfect and please everyone and everything around us can create a perceived feeling of safety and necessity. We feel like we are needed and wanted, and that we are adding value to our life and to others around us.

The truth of the matter is, that when we fall into this trap, we add more stress and pressure to our life because perfectionism is both unobtainable and already obtained at the same time. We are divinely, messily and perfectly human and we don't need to change. The stories we create, however, require us to think that we're not good enough, worthy enough, or loveable just as we are, and that we need to take action to ensure others don't 'find us out'.

'My Best Is Good Enough' is the statement I use in clinic to test the stress of perfection held within my clients. Technically, the answer we should get from the body is *'Yes, I am doing my best, my best is good enough and I am ok as I am.'*

Clearly, with our internal landscape and conditioning, this is rarely the case.

The second question to back it up is the percentage to which we state that it is true - *'My Best is 100%'*. All we can ever give is 100% of what we have to offer, so that also *should* test as a strong, positive answer.

Regularly, this percentage heads into the thousands, which equates to a problem. If your *'My best is 100%'* tests up at say 4,700%, it means that you are trying to do the work of, and be, 47 perfect people to consider yourself good enough in your own life. Each perfect person we are striving to be equates to 100%.

In essence, with the above example, we are trying to live up to 47 people's ideas and ideals of perfectionism. If we assume that each of those people are holding a rule book containing their ideals of perfection, they are probably each carrying a tome the size of *War and Peace* all with exhaustive ideas of what 'perfect' means.

Therefore, we are trying to live up to 47 rule books of perfection, each containing conflicting and different rules and measures for what perfect is. Exhausting much?

The actions we take when we look externally for ideal perfection, create a huge amount of stress and pressure on the body. We are living up to standards which don't exist and can't be achieved by anyone.

Our nervous system is constantly on the lookout for threats to our perfection. And, knowing that we can't live up to that causes our Reticular Activating System (RAS) to go into overdrive by bringing everything that disproves our perfection into our consciousness.

What an endlessly tiring cycle. This constant drive for perfection mixed with people-pleasing and a dash of fixing all the problems of the world is often the underlying cause of exhaustion, adrenal dysfunction, anxiety, and other nervous system disorders.

Our job is to learn to throw out everybody else's rule books. Create a bonfire with them if you must. But get rid of them. Tune into your heart and soul, and replace all of those rule books with one simple question:

What's in my Highest Good RIGHT NOW?

This is actually one of the only questions you need to direct your internal compass. It removes so much external stress and pressure from your life.

Your ideal of perfection changes from moment to moment and has multiple external influences - your energy levels, how much sleep you got, the weather, and so much more. Therefore, your perfect meal today will change tomorrow and the next day, as will everything you need for your internal growth, needs and wants, and your external requirements for work, relationships and roles you fulfil.

Your 'Highest Good' can never be detrimental to others.

Even if they perceive it as such, your Highest Good takes into account that we are all inextricably linked within the fabric of the Oneness of the Universe. If you operate at your Highest Purpose and bring it into the world, it can only be beneficial to others.

Think about experiencing a long day at work, then going home to cook dinner. You know you have ingredients for a healthy salad in the fridge, but you're tired and don't have the energy to make it.

What will be in the Highest Good for you in that *moment?*

If you go home and cut up salad with resentment and anger, guess what's going into the food? Yep, resentment and anger! And everyone eats a harder-to-digest meal even though, in theory, it's healthier.

If you stop at the fish and chip shop on the way home and pick up takeaway, then plonk it in the middle of the table at home, you remove the associated stress. And the food you digest could actually have a greater overall benefit.

Instead of a healthy salad laden with resentment and anger dressing, you ingest a meal without stress, pressure and negativity.

Believe it or not, on the odd occasion, that will be the 'perfect' meal. When I've done this, my family thinks I'm the *best* for bringing home a treat, I feel less stressed, and we all sit around and have a laugh.

Sometimes, this is the healthier option. Reduction of stress, increased relaxation, and greater connection can actually improve our digestion as our emotional, spiritual, social, mental and energetic selves are all being nourished and nurtured. The physical body can certainly better digest a less healthy meal when there is an increase in goodness for those other aspects.

Other times, you may well be prepared to cut up that salad knowing that you need the goodness within, so you are in full clarity about the option you choose.

Whichever choice you make, if it is in your Highest Good, right in that moment it will be the perfect choice for you. And the overall benefits will be in everyone's favour.

This is the full feeling into and discernment around *'What's in my Highest Good right now?'* It takes away our reliance on external sources and brings the power fully back to us. Internal truth over external influence.

Life changes when we trust our internal compass, act on the messages we receive, and keep coming back to our heart and soul. It has no other choice.

The Three-Legged Stool

Thoughts, emotions and behaviours are like the legs of a three-legged stool. When one is affected, the stool is unbalanced, unstable and likely to fall under pressure, if it stands up at all. When we want to change one of the three, we need to work on all three aspects and understand the underlying thoughts and emotions which are reflected in externalised behaviours, and how they influence each other. When we are less conscious of our behavioural patterns, thoughts and emotions, we are unsure which affects which.

Dr Joe Dispenza once said:

The same thoughts always lead to the same choices. Same choices lead to the same behaviours. The same behaviours lead to the same experiences, and the same experiences produce the same emotions. And these emotions drive the very same thoughts.

As you can see, we get stuck in an unconscious loop that can be challenging to recognise. And what we can't recognise, we have difficulty changing because it is our 'normal'. Repeated cycles, outcomes and arguments are actually fantastic signposts of where we can start delving into our desire to change our life.

These cyclical behaviours often keep us in our comfort zone, which is often anything but comfortable. Our repetition of behaviours, thoughts and emotions can keep us stuck in negative cycles and cause pain to our psyche and physical body. Thinking about the comfort zone as the *'known'* zone, gives it more clarity, and is a more apt description.

Our known zone is the place we know. We feel safe because we repeat ingrained behaviours and do not push ourselves to change, grow and learn new patterns and ways of relating. We assume that, because we remain in our tribe, we are, at a minimum, safe. When we realise that the known zone is actually painful and creates disturbance, dis-ease and a lack of wellness in our life, and the pain of staying the same becomes greater than the pain and discomfort of change, we start looking for ways to heal, change and grow. As the poet Anais Nin says:

And the day came when the risk to remain tight in a bud was more painful than the risk it took to blossom.

Different healing modalities start with different legs of the stool. Start your process from wherever you feel most drawn. If you notice behaviours that are repetitively getting you into trouble, arguments and emotional turmoil, start there. If your thought patterns weigh you down and send you into a spiral of negativity, then that may be the place to start. And if you experience emotional outbursts, imbalance and disharmony, then look at them.

We regularly keep ourselves in boxes of our own making with labels we've collected over the years. The stories we attach to during our lives, based on insults, comments and conditioning, form our experience and influence which labels we own and wear. Those labels dictate who we are to be in the world, whilst other labels which are handed to us are discarded as unfitting and not for us.

For example, when I was very young, people used to say that mum was stopped in the street to say how beautiful my sister was, yet I was 'cute'. I was told that cute is what they call a baby if they're ugly and don't want to offend the parent. Add to that the continual comments about my height throughout my formative years and, wow, talk about carrying baggage about my physical appearance. I embodied those stories and struggled deeply with self-hatred about my looks well into my late 30s. The thoughts about my body influenced the emotions I felt and the behaviours I exhibited. They were not exclusive and operating alone, they were a big tangled web of negativity and yuck.

At school, (and by my first romantic partner), I was also often told that my sister was the 'smart' one, the 'funny' one, the 'pretty' one. As a result, I, in my black and white, child and teen-based thinking, gave myself the opposite labels and behaved as though they were true. I was the dumb, fat, ugly one. I was stupid and knew little. In fact, in the middle of high school, I even changed from maths-focused subjects to humanities-based subjects so I couldn't be compared as easily.

None of this was anybody's fault, but it is a great example of how we take what people say and create stories, labels and personalities that we then live out as though they are the truth. But, as we learned earlier, the truth has 144 sides and what I made into my truth was, in fact, only the opinions of a few people.

Compliments were met with disbelief, layers of hurt and a form of hidden, passive or outright aggression. It was easier to bring in and feel anger and disbelief than to look at the hurt that sat underneath, exacerbating my internal sense of unworthiness, ugliness and unloveability.

Feeling divided, I had an external aggressor who protected a vulnerable, open-wounded child beneath. Behavioural personas were created to protect my inner softness and sensitivity, which felt too unprotected and misunderstood. The world never felt safe for a true, authentic version of myself to emerge and show my face and heart.

Once looking from the *'three-legged stool'* perspective, I became clearly aware that I could start at any leg and find myself in a place where I could heal. My externalised behaviours were the end result of unhealthy thought patterns and a lack of emotional regulation which desperately needed to be fine tuned by education, awareness and self-compassion when I slipped back into learned habits.

This externalised behaviour was often all or nothing, a blazing fire or angry smouldering, neither of which were helpful. When they weren't being used, my only choice was disconnection and distraction.

The visual of a three-legged stool gives us an ability to work on all three, simultaneously gaining deep understanding as we dive into the leg that feels best as a starting point.

Emotional Fluency

Emotional fluency is a vital part of personal and spiritual development.

Emotional fluency doesn't mean that life is always happiness and positivity. It's actually quite the opposite. It means that you experience ALL emotions without holding onto prejudice or judgement for what you feel, which allows the responses to be named and acknowledged. You work through the discomfort (yes, even positive emotions can create discomfort) and then either release the emotion, move through stuckness, or hold onto it a little longer to understand it better.

These days we are rarely connected to our emotions. We busily distract ourselves with work, family, friends, Netflix, Facebook, TikTok, and so much more besides. 'Busyness' is worn like a badge of honour.

We are seen as a mind with a body, rather than a body with a soul and, as a result, we live in our heads. We think through how we are and 'should' be rather than feel into it with our bodily intelligence. We construct stories about why we feel the way we do, and consciously or subconsciously suppress the way we feel so that we don't express our feelings in the wrong way, which will lead to rejection from the tribe and 'death'.

More often we get asked what we *think* about something rather than how we feel about it. *'Thinking'* is seen as Monarch, with *'emoting'* as its poorer cousin.

To feel, be present and become emotionally fluent, we need to fully come out of our heads and connect into our bodies.

We can't think our way into feelings, and can't rationalise and 'logic' them either. The conscious mind is not equipped to think around emotional problems. We need to feel our way through. Scary, but necessary.

Emotions are simply energy in motion. They are energetic messages we receive from our body to tell us whether we are heading towards something we want more or less of. Yet we often ignore the messages we get, if we notice them at all through the busyness. We are often too preoccupied to spend any time connecting into the feelings that course through our veins and influence our externalised behaviours.

According to Cyndi Dale in *Energetic Boundaries*:

A belief is a perception about reality. A feeling is a message from our body. Beliefs tell us what feelings we should feel, and our feelings tell us what to do with our beliefs.

Feelings and emotions are intricately linked with our belief systems. The physical visceral responses that memories and subconscious programming raise in our bodies often feel as real as they did when we experienced the original event. Our beliefs often register as truths to which we live, yet can simply be off kilter programmes that are past their use-by date.

We judge our emotions harshly, and have lofty expectations of what life should be. Within the ups and downs of life, we often want to sit on the happy side of normal range. The extremes of joy and depression are often areas that we want to steer away from.

Think of the worst moments of your life.

Did that emotion stay forever, or did it dissipate and change over time?
When you go to your highest highs, do you remain there?

All emotions are transitory, but society and conditioning often tells us to *'Make hay while the sun shines'* or *'Enjoy it while it lasts'*. This ingrains the beliefs that good emotions are fleeting and won't last, the joy thief will be right along to ruin our good fortune, but bad emotions will hang around to make our lives miserable.

Once we befriend that emotional fluctuation and understand its impermanence, we become more comfortable naming each of the emotions we feel, and using them as guideposts rather than finite 'This is it' indicators.

Mad, Sad and Glad

Most people live with and identify only three major emotions - mad, sad and glad. It's amazing how the wide gamut of what we feel can be reduced to such a small range of emotional descriptors. In doing so, we are trying to simplify the unsimplifiable whilst prioritising rationality and ignoring the full expression of emotion, feeling and experience.

Emotional fluency helps people take those three emotional states and use them like the primary colours, a base to create differentiation and greater fluency; to give shade and texture, life and depth to the internal landscape of our emotional world and embodied experience. When we reconnect to the full range of greys from black to white, and our entire Pantone colour chart, our traumas heal, life expands and we grow. Rather than stunting growth with limited expressions, being aware of the enhanced texture and shade of our feelings amplifies our experiences and expands our emotional fluency to bring much appreciated insight and change.

The first stage of learning emotional fluency is to drop into our body and become present, so that we read our current landscape, not one from the past or an imagined one from the future.

Once fully present, we separate ourselves from the emotion. When we feel emotions and say *'I am angry/sad/happy'*, we are saying that we are the emotion, that there is no room for anything else to be present and exist within us. We are one with the emotion, which is untrue. To come back to the pure state of truth, we need to put distance between the emotion and ourselves.

We are a soul in a body having a human experience of feeling emotions and rolling in the messiness of humanity.

Rather than *'I am'*, try to substitute *'I feel'* before the emotion. This gives us space to allow more of who and what we actually are to enter the picture and be acknowledged. If that doesn't give you enough space, try to speak of yourself in the third person and bring in the compassion from your inner best friend - *'Amanda is feeling angry/sad/happy/etc.'* These techniques bring us into being the observer of our emotions rather than being the emotion itself.

If someone you love says *'I'm feeling angry'*, how do you respond? You'd probably ask what is causing it, whether they need support, or if they need a hug? You'd employ love and compassion.

Speaking of your feelings in the third person can evoke a similarly compassionate response, which makes it easier to:
- Identify what you are feeling
- Understand why you are feeling it
- Start to look at what you might need to move forward (solving the problem or sitting with it a little longer).

There are not enough words to describe the feelings of the soul. Even with increased emotional fluency and the ability to bring a multitude of words into the picture, it can feel like human language fails at times to give the full expression to our experience and emotional landscape. When we acknowledge that, we are able to move to another emotional state.

Let's look at an example of an emotion and how we can build colour, texture and context around it.

Anger is one of my favourite emotions to work with. If we take the time to reflect on anger and delve deeper, it can tell us so much about our emotional state.

Anger tells us when:
- Our boundaries have been crossed
- We feel powerless or hurt
- We are afraid
- We feel big, deep emotions such as unloved, disconnected, disrespected, rejected or abandoned.

Frustration, a shade of anger, helps to tell us when we are not in alignment and congruence with our desired inner state and our life purpose.

Dr Brené Brown's research has shown that:

It's easier to feel pissed off than hurt.

Humans often want to express anger rather than investigate hurt because it causes pain to explore 'hurt'. Expressing anger allows us a release, a projection of blame and a temporary relief from the internal feeling.

When we have the courage to look beneath the anger to the root cause, we can often see, on a much deeper level, where we are going. It can demonstrate when we are off our path, if we are living to external influences, and if we prioritise things in our life that do not lead us towards our purpose.

When we are in anger, we are not able to look beneath it.

The physiological reaction that comes with anger moves us from our creative front brain (where we are able to think rationally, self-monitor, engage our personality, plan, and organise) into our back brain survival mode.

Anger also has many shades we can use to give it more texture, description and understanding. At one end of the spectrum, we can feel mild irritation and annoyance, with full blown rage and wrath at the other. There are multiple variables and root causes within one emotion, and multiple ways to deal with it, gain awareness of what it means for us and, therefore, greater ways we can befriend it and understand its reason for being.

It's important to note that resentment is not part of the anger family but, instead, belongs to a different emotional family where envy sits. When we feel resentment, we are often envious that others have the freedom to do as they wish. We give and give and give - to family, work or other commitments - and we resent seeing others, who are not giving as much, daring to set boundaries and take time for themselves, and making sure their needs are met and cared for.

Such as we've done for anger, we can create a spectrum with any other emotion. We can dig beneath any emotion that we are feeling for our root cause emotion, circumstance, emotional trigger or situation that is causing the disharmony.

Emotions can behave like toddlers - they want to be the centre of attention.

Emotions will do anything to get noticed; they will pull at your sleeve, tug at your leg, call your name and poke you until there is a reaction. Sometimes when we ignore them long enough, they may lash out at others, or create disturbance to ensure they have our full, undivided attention.

They often want nothing other than acknowledgement and validation of their existence, so they can run off happy and blissfully unaware of the full extent of annoyance they've caused with their perceived bothersome persistence.

Emotional fluency gives you words and feelings to acknowledge what you may not have recognised before. As you acknowledge what you are feeling and validate why that feeling exists in your body, then you have a choice to stay with it for a while, or shift out of it and change it into the next best feeling emotion. You are also able to make a date with it for later on if the reason you are unable to stay with it is an inappropriate situation (for example, feeling deep grief at work). That way, the emotion still feels seen, heard, acknowledged and validated.

The more safe you feel in your body, and the more you work on cultivating that feeling of safety to be an easily accessible place within you, the safer it becomes to express and process your emotions.

This gives you an emotional freedom that many only dream of, and releases you from the emotional addictions of the past.

When we use this acknowledgement and validation of emotions, they are able to move through the body rather than get stuck as they do when we avoid, ignore, suppress or repress them.

To survive in the world, we often deny the full expression of positive emotions.
We reject the experience of full rapturous joy, in the expectation that it could be taken from us at any minute. Our 'joy thief' comes in saying *'Who are you to be so happy? What if things fall apart?'*

When we numb one end of the emotional spectrum, we can't help but numb the whole spectrum. We cannot selectively numb feelings - *'Ooh, this one's good, give me more of this, but I'll ignore and deny my experience of that.'*

Turning to numbing to deny the emotional landscape within us is a deeply learned behaviour. When we've been conditioned since childhood to ignore our internal emotional state and only operate within a thin band of socially acceptable emotions, anything else constitutes a failure on our part and becomes something we are often shamed and humiliated for.

Think back to when 'little you' fell over. Do you remember being told, *'Get up. Get on with it. There's no blood, you're fine?'*

We are told to dust ourselves off and harden the fuck up (that one usually comes a little later but is no less prominent). What if, right in that moment, you want to acknowledge the pain in your knee, the embarrassment of falling over, the hurt, and any other emotion that may be coursing through your body?

And what if you want to cry and allow a release of some of that emotional build up? Why is that seen as so shameful and wrong? How many times have you heard, *'You're such a baby. Only babies cry. You're a big girl/boy. You'll be ok. It's not so bad.'*

Who are they to tell you what you feel inside?
Who are they to judge your reactions to YOUR fucking pain?
Why do they get to shame and embarrass you for hurting and feeling deeply?

When we deny our experience of emotions as children, we are being programmed to ignore our feelings across the full scale spectrum. We learn to deny our own emotional wisdom, and we often create internal stories that suggest we are overreacting, too sensitive, a 'sook' or a baby.

God knows that we don't intend to create those story lines within our children or ourselves, but that is the conditioning that we encourage when we deny the true and full expression of emotions and the inner landscape which nurtures the emotional Self.

Adults do this denial of feelings, not out of spite or with intention to damage children, but through passing on their conditioning and programming. Don't think I'm immune to that, by the way. I know how much I've damaged my children with the conditioning within me, and I pray that they too are able to learn from the growth and inner work I've done to encourage their own sense of Self and acceptance of all parts of who they are.

Think of all the times we are told when we are young that we're too sensitive, we need thicker skin, we aren't taking that joke the way it was intended, or that we're 'too much' or 'not enough' of what's 'acceptable'.

But what if that joke hurts?

What if something we're not sensitive to is a point of real pain for the person on the receiving end? Sometimes others make jokes that hurt.

Who decides what hurts another and what doesn't?
Who gets to deny someone's feelings in any situation?
Why do we get to deny the other person's hurt and not take grown-up responsibility for creating that hurt in them?

Each internalised denial shuts us down. Shame and embarrassment makes us hide emotions and those spiritual parts of ourselves. We shy away from showing those intimate and sensitive parts to protect ourselves from pain.

It is often people we inherently trust who can be the most judgemental and comment on our life, choices, and decisions.

These influential people don't always remember that we are separate from them, that we have different lives to live and our own unique path to walk. In most cases, this conditioning is done by those who want to keep us safe, love us and guide us in a way that protects us in the world.

But only we know what is in our Highest Good. The more we tap into that, the more we can express that in the world with freedom and without self-judgement.

The Paradox of Conflicting Emotions

Paradoxically, we can experience a multitude of conflicting emotions at the same time and have all of them be completely true. This does not always fit in the *'right versus wrong'* duality that we often try to work in when we think our way through life. Our brains love oppositions and struggle to understand the both/and concept of multiple truths being true at the same time.

Emotional regulation is not about not feeling or expressing emotions. It is about not letting the emotional state have power over you. Unprocessed emotions become like an ever-growing cancer and, at some point, we need to unpack, process and heal them to be able to move forward with clarity, lightness and embodied healing.

It takes a great deal of courage and vulnerability to befriend our emotions. Leaning into emotions, particularly on either end of the spectrum, can feel like the last thing you want to do. But, as you practice, the more you understand and reap the benefits.

I suggest deeply grounding your energy, keeping two feet on the ground and gently leaning in with inquisitiveness and curiosity.

We don't always need to leap off a cliff and swan dive into the tumultuous waves of our emotions and the resulting uncertainty they create beneath us. A gentle approach can give us more grounded certainty, strength and conviction to lean gently into the scary landscape ahead.

Our emotions and vulnerability, supported by appropriate boundaries, give us facets of toughness, strength and courage which allow us to live more wholeheartedly and in alignment with our values, ethics and morals.

In owning our emotional landscape and leaning in with courage and vulnerability to pain, we are able to unhook from the traumas of our past and rebuild our relationships with Self and others. Our emotional landscapes become wonderful tapestries of light and dark, shadows and highlights, and are able to tell a story of full brilliance, pain and everything in between. *What could be more magical than that?*

I wore blame like a heavy cloak. My younger self attempted to suppress, ignore and demean most of my emotions. They felt unsafe and, when I did show them in their full glory, I often felt shame, blame or disdain was given to me. Super emotional for as long as I can remember, despite trying to hide it, I wear my heart on my sleeve for all to see and, as a result, have regularly been taken advantage of. Always wanting to please others, many could sense my need to be liked and the desire to gratify others at cost to myself. Because of this, I attracted those who teased, bullied and, later, abused me; I was an easy target for nastiness. I was told regularly that I couldn't take a joke, needed thicker skin and that I was too emotional. Nobody ever seemed to take responsibility for saying hurtful things or causing harm, the blame was always pushed back onto me... and I took it. I wore it like a heavy cloak. Over time it wore me down.

Eventually, due to all that suppressed emotion, I became an angry, ready to erupt volcano.

There was no room to squash anything else down. I was full, hurting, hated myself with a passion and was heading into depression. I felt unloved, unheard, unseen, disrespected and like I didn't matter to anyone.

I used to blame my reactions and defensiveness on being an Aries who used the fire within to burn bridges left, right and centre. Before I started the journey to become an Alchemist, I either felt like I was a smouldering fire or exploding like Mt Vesuvius. I never managed to find a healthy balance and thought everybody else held the controls. Spoiler alert - they didn't, I did!

Through building an internal personal and spiritual connection I've learned to be less reactive.

I have a strong bond with the safe harbour within myself so that, even when life is tumultuous and feels like it's 'against me', I have the capacity to find love, compassion and acceptance (not always with understanding) for myself and others. I am now able to remain connected to myself, my wants and needs whilst in communion with others.

We have the full ability to control our internal navigation systems and thermostats. Oftentimes, we react without conscious awareness because of built up emotional tension and a lack of processing.

Reactions, activations and triggering within our body are usually due to pent up, unexpressed, and often overwhelming emotions. As we practice with our Emotional Fluency, this activation becomes more neutral. We are more readily able to see what led to the build up and take responsibility for our part in it. We become the observer of the emotion and the emotional state rather than feeling like we are the emotion itself.

Exercises: Building Emotional Fluency

Feeling Emotional Weight

An easy exercise for you to practice recognising the weight of emotions.

First, feel into anger, sadness or grief.
What do they feel like in your body?
Are they heavy? These emotions can feel heavy as they vibrate at a slower rate.

Now feel into love, joy, and happiness.
What do they feel like?
They are of a Higher vibration, move faster and, therefore, feel lighter.

Acknowledge and Validate > Shift or Stay?

What name, or names, do you give to the feeling you have in your body right now? Remember that multiple emotions can exist simultaneously. (For some great resources that help you expand your emotional awareness with words for emotions, search 'emotion charts' online. These give colour, texture and life to emotions, rather than limiting us to the emotional terms we use regularly).

Can you find a better description than the one you originally used?
How does it feel in your body?
What does it need from you?

This may just be acknowledgement and validation. Or there may be an action you need to take. It could be that you simply need to sit with the emotion for a while and do nothing. In other words, do you need to do something to shift out of it, or to allow some time for it to just be there?

Journal Prompts

Take a few deep breaths, settle into your body and feel deeply within. What's going on? What do you feel, right now in this moment?

Start by giving the most prominent feeling a name.

What shades of that emotion/feeling exist? Can you add more texture and depth to what you've described so far?

Can you reduce the overall description into something more fitting?

How does the emotion feel in your body?
  Is it heavy or light? Is it spiky or smooth? Does it have a texture, shape or colour?

What happens when you tune into it? Do you get more answers of why the emotion is sitting there?

What's sitting underneath the emotion that you're feeling? Why is that there?

What's underneath that? What message does it have for you?

Self-Love: Gritty and Real

Slowly, tentatively, like a foal on unsteady legs
Not sure which foot to put where, but knowing that trying is the only option
Surely it will get easier

Gradually, step by shaky step, peeling back the layers
The unworthiness
The lack of loveability
The too muchness
The fear
The hurt
The projections
And when you finally hit the core, keep going!

Peeling and shedding
Stripping back who they want you to be
Removing the cloak that allowed you to fit into their perfect world
Removing all illusions, smoke and mirrors that you are like them
Allowing your soul to be fully exposed to the world

New, naked and vulnerable
Yet real, connected and true
Still stumbling at times, learning the steps
Finding the new tunes to which you can dance
But gaining in confidence every single day

Trust in the self
And knowingness that there is something greater than the small self out there
Pushing you forward
Cheering you on
Silent, invisible, universal support

You may not own all that they think is beautiful
Or right
Or perfect
Being true to yourself is the only way to proceed

Shine your unique beauty
Your poise
Dignity
Grace
And all the messiness and imperfections alongside

The difference between then and now?
Being filled with love, acceptance and joy
In the stripping bare you can be more you than ever before
And that is something worth loving
Wholeheartedly and with gratitude

No more apologies
No more will pieces be sliced off to fit in their perfect box

Self-love is not rainbows, unicorns, fluffy memes and social media bullshit.

Self-love is hard decisions, strong boundaries, deeply knowing yourself, and being discerning about what is right and wrong for you right now, in this exact moment.

Self-love is saying *'No'* when you need to and enforcing that 'no' in the way that your body needs in that moment.

Self-love is gritty and challenging as hell. It is self-responsibility in life, love and healing. It is certainly not for the faint of heart, but every step is worthy, wonderful, and brings magic to your world.

Memes and social media posts from influencers and the like show self-love as light, airy, fun….it reminds me of the old style period advertisements on TV where women in white trousers ride horses along the beach, play tennis and have a grand old time without a care in the world. *What the actual fuck?* The reality is so different.

Self-love is discernment about what's acceptable and what's not acceptable from ourselves, towards ourselves, and from others towards us. Healthy boundaries, honest and encouraging self-talk, learning to be 'of' service to rather than 'in' service to, and cultivating compassion, acceptance and honesty towards yourself, are all valuable learnings as you navigate the path towards self-love.

Self-love asks us to honour our shadows and our light, to allow us to build trust between our conscious and subconscious mind, and to acknowledge the reality of the situation as we see it. Discernment is key as we delve into the heart of the matter, read the innermost intricacies, and learn to mark the differences between what we let in and what we need to keep out.

Finally, self-love also encompasses how we show up to our relationships, whether intimate, closely connected, or with mere acquaintances. The way we show up tells others a lot about how we value ourselves and what we are willing to accept from them within the confines of our connection.

The more you learn to love and accept yourself, the more you are able to let love into your life. As you increase self-love, you see what works for you, and what doesn't. You build a catalogue of experience which demonstrates where past behaviours have taken you, and you are able to create an 'evidence library' that shows what you desire more of in your life, and what you want to remove.

You will learn that it is ok to 'choose yourself' and put yourself first. Then, that grows to become a priority of choosing yourself and your internal truth over others and their external influence.

At the end of the day, we need to love ourselves first and foremost, because we are the ones we spend every minute of every day with. It makes life a much more pleasant experience if we spend that time with someone we love, despite our faults, rather than someone we dislike, or even hate.

Building the catalogue of experience also builds trust that we will make the right decision and that, when we don't, we will have a lesson to learn, more subconscious clearing to do, or a new layer of the onion to unpeel.

Boundaries

Boundaries are, according to the online Cambridge Dictionary:

A real or imagined line that marks the edge or limit of something; the limit of a subject or principle; and the limit of what someone considers to be acceptable behaviour.

Oftentimes, when we are newly acquainted with boundaries, we put hard edges in place. We can become a *'boundary bully'*, enforcing our boundaries without regard for situational difference, our mood, energy or context. We create walls, fences and turrets with the idea of safe-guarding ourselves from harm. Creating such strong boundaries can backfire on us if we cut ourselves off from connection with others. If this happens, we need to reassess, soften where needed and discern which boundaries need to stay strong, and which can become more of a dance.

Boundaries play a vital role in our life and relationships. If you haven't had many boundaries in the past, when you first start putting them in and exercising them, those who have benefitted from you not having any will often push back and have problems with the 'new you'.

A boundary is simply a line that says what is ok and what is not ok. I love the quote from Prentis Hemphill who says:

Boundaries are the distance at which I can love you and me simultaneously.

How I wished I learned that earlier. Instead, I spent all my time giving everything I had on every level of my being to everyone else, without keeping anything for myself. Exhausted by trying to make myself fit into everyone else's boxes, my illnesses and dis-ease were also the turning point for me to learn to choose me first, so that I had something to give others.

Boundaries ebb and flow with our mood, sleep, energy levels, the closeness of the relationships in which we are setting them, and many other factors besides. Some days, we will have the energy to allow more flexibility, and other days we may be more rigid. Whatever we choose to enforce is ok, it is perfect for where we are right then. We are in control of them, no-one else.

Setting boundaries is often the easy part. Enforcing them with healthy consequences can be more tricky.

Once we have decided where our edges lie, we need to practice with our comfort of enforcing them and creating consequences for boundary violations. A relatively easy way to know if our boundaries have been violated is to monitor our anger in response.

Other people will react to our boundaries, especially if we haven't had them before. They will respond with anger, disappointment and a whole range of emotions when we set boundaries. Our challenge comes in enforcing them when we know that they disapprove.

As we gain proficiency in setting and enforcing, boundaries become more of a dance where we are in a position to set them and move them as our needs arise. Firm, hard and immovable boundaries will still be necessary in certain areas of our lives, but those will often be energetically held once the underlying work is done because we raise our vibration to a state where that behaviour is no longer a match for our energetic signal.

Accept and honour other people's boundaries. While we think about what is ok for us and where to draw our lines in the sand, we often don't consider where other people's lines fall.

As we work on recognising our triggers and activations, we also learn that other people's boundaries are not about us. They are keeping themselves safe, happy and supported by recognising and acknowledging their wants and needs.

Can we practice being ok with that and not take it personally? Can we encourage their identification of boundaried behaviour even when it doesn't suit us?

Exercise: Creating Boundaries

Saying a Divine No

Learning to say 'No' can be challenging. We often want to say 'Yes' to keep others happy and to 'guarantee' our connection. Sometimes, 'Yes' is the wrong answer for our heart and soul.

So, how do we say 'No'?

When we tune in deeply to our wants, needs and desires, and feel into our heart and soul, answers become clear.

As we practice our noes, we become more attuned to how they sit within the body. Some noes feel uncomfortable but give us more than we lose by saying them. Some noes feel immediately great within us, and others don't necessarily give us clarity on their rightness or wrongness until later. This is where practice and honest reflection become a vital part of our growth.

An example, if your boss tries to give you a project and your workload is crazy full, you know that if you say 'Yes', you'll be working all the hours God sends, and more, to get the work done on time and on task. Not to mention potentially not doing your own workload as you prioritise the work they have requested. The work you do won't be the best quality when you rush, work while tired, and probably do a half-arsed job with resentment flowing in your veins.

Now, imagine tuning into that and saying, *'Thank you for thinking of me, but I don't have the capacity for that right now. If we can find someone to hand my current work over to, then perhaps I can fit it in, but without support, it's a No.'*

Encouraging bosses will hear that, appreciate the openness and honesty, and take the project to the next person on their list. But many people wouldn't dare approach their boss with that openness and clarity through fear of losing their job, being ill thought of, or habitual *'Yes'* programming.

> *Saying a Divine No helps you say 'Yes' to yourself, your needs and wants, and your energy levels.*

At other times, our Divine No may actually be a *'Not Right Now'* - *'I can't do that today, but perhaps I could on Tuesday. Does that work for you?'* Or *'I can't help you this time, but next time you need someone, please call on me because I'd love to help you.'*

To quote Brené Brown once again:

> *Clear is kind, unclear is unkind.*

Self-Talk

What does your inner dialogue sound like? Is it encouraging and loving? Or self-critical and demeaning?

Until my late 30's, I hated myself. I hated the way I looked, the way I acted, how much I drank, and how I sometimes acted when I was drunk. I especially hated the way I denied myself being me. It got so bad towards the end of my 'past life' (pre-spiritual awakening), that

I used to want to smash mirrors when I caught sight of myself. I knew I'd been lying to myself for as long as I could remember about who I was, what I wanted, and the health of my relationships. The sight of that person made me sick.

My self-talk was vile, hate-filled and would have made people cringe had it been played out of a mega phone on the top of my head. I was, far and away, my biggest abuser, and thought I deserved all the abuse dished out to me, by myself and others.

Many people have a naturally self-critical inner voice. As humans, we are all predisposed to negativity and speak to ourselves in ways we wouldn't speak to our worst enemy, let alone our loved ones. The 'itty bitty shitty committee' inside us loves to keep a running dialogue of what we're doing wrong, how everyone is better than us and how we could improve if only we weren't so fat, stupid, ugly….(fill in your own favourite self-flagellating term here).

Our inner talk is such an entrenched part of our psyche that we are often unaware of its negative and constant commentary. In fact, when clients are asked about it, they often tell me their inner voice is fine, encouraging, and not too bad. But, as they become more aware, the opposite is regularly found to be true.

When working in Kinesiology, we set up different indicator muscles, one of which is a yes/no.

While setting up this response, I specify *'show me 100% yes'*, anything less is a hard no from the body. This indicator is vital to my success in balancing a client because, even if something is more than 99.999% true, if there is any shadow of doubt standing in the way of '100% yes', then it tests as a 'No'.

I use this analogy to help clients reframe their inner voice. (Yes, this is a long-term, ongoing practice and doesn't stop after a week or two of awareness.) When they are in the midst of chastising themselves, putting themselves down, or downright abusing themselves, I work with them to be aware of what they are saying internally.

They then ask themselves *'Is it true?'* If there is even the slightest doubt, (spoiler alert - if it's negative self-talk, it's never true), they practice reframing to something that feels true for them.

To increase their awareness, they imagine a megaphone sitting on their crown chakra that broadcasts their inner voice to the world. If they're proud of it, that's great, there's no work to be done. If they're not, then the practice needs to continue. So far, I've not met too many people who would be 100% happy with the megaphone installation.

In addition, I ask clients if they would speak to their loved ones the way they speak to themselves. Once again, I've never met anyone who has said yes to this.

Make contact with your inner best friend, inner wise person, and inner encouragers. These people may speak firmly to you if you're out of line, but they will always speak to you with love, encouragement, acceptance and compassion.

The most inspirational turnaround with a client working on self-talk and self-love was a young person I worked with one year at a festival. With only 15 minutes to do a mini-balance, I wondered *'How the fuck am I going to make a difference with so little time?'* I prayed and sent my intention for Spirit to flow through me and allow deep healing to occur.

This young person was filled with self-hatred and had self-harm marks up their arms. With young children myself, the mother in me wanted to hug and protect them to make sure they were never again harmed. I know their parents felt the same way.

We talked about self-love and how important they were as a unique soul. When they spoke of what others thought about them at school, I said:

Unless we check in with people, we don't know what they are thinking about us. That person you think is giving you funny looks, may not be thinking about you at all. You are perceiving them looking back at you with your perception of self. But you have your own unique perceptions, life views, belief systems, experiences and conditioning, and have your own negative self-talk that you are putting into their head. All you are doing, in that moment, is perceiving their perception of you. How far from the truth do you think that puts you? Most people think about themselves more than others, so they are more than likely looking at you and doing the same thing.

For homework I asked them to start recognising their inner voice and, when they are stuck in negative self-talk to reframe into a more positive inner voice. They also needed to practice saying *'I love you'* into a mirror while looking deep into their own eyes and pure soul.

When they left, I didn't know if I'd ever see them again but, fast forward a year, and they were once again at the festival. They were changed. They hadn't self-harmed since our initial meeting, their internal voice was more noticeably positive and they had a more settled confidence. Their energy field had also transformed. While the humanness of them still had doubt and other negative feelings towards Self, they were more in control and happier within.

I remember asking them and their parent for permission to hug them both. We all hugged with tears in our eyes, happy with the turn around and result of our cumulative work together.

While I was the practitioner here, all the work was done by the client. They chose to take what was said into their being and recognise the truth in it. They did the daily work to recognise the less than desirable habits and to choose an alternate way of being.

A flip slide to understanding your self-talk is also understanding what to take on when others throw their perceptions, projections and other 'stuff' at you.

One of my clients was going through a nasty divorce and had received some emails from their ex, accusing them of being a poor role model for their children. There was a barrage of other insults and nastiness in the email that, understandably, brought up a huge plethora of emotions.

This is where we can use our question of 'Is it true?'

If you receive something similar, allow your initial emotion to be felt and the rawness to subside, (it's important to release your immediate emotions to do this exercise).

Then, 24-48 hours later, go back and read over it with more objectivity, (if it was face-to-face interaction, take some time to think back over it). As you read each insult or activation of emotion, *feel into it*.

Does it feel true for you?
Does it feel like your stuff or theirs?
Does some of it hit home as your truth?

If it feels like it doesn't belong to you, and activates any emotional triggers that belong to you, leave it where it needs to be - on the page and out of your psyche. If something has hit home, play with it and see what attention it needs.

Does it need healing?
Does it have a message for you?
Is it a behaviour/trait/etc that actually serves you well and requires tweaking rather than healing?

This exercise holds great power. The quantity of shit we accept from others diminishes when we are able to do this successfully. Their opinions, truth and thoughts are exactly that - theirs. Do you need to own their stuff and yours? I suggest no.

Exercise: Access your Inner Wise Person, Best Friend and Encouragers

To access them, bring yourself back to your body with 3-4 deep belly breaths. Consciously slow your breathing down. Take the breath in as deeply as you can, feeling your diaphragm (the muscle at the bottom of your rib cage) expand.

Putting your hand on your belly can give you something to aim for when you are breathing to make sure the breath is not high up in your chest. If it feels right for you, add a hand to your heart space too.

Feel your belly move in and out as you breathe.

Breathe in and out for the same number of counts, holding for one or two counts at the top and bottom. You may need to start with a number as low as two, i.e., in for two, hold for one, out for two, hold for one. Work your way up to six-eight counts in, hold for two, out for six-eight, hold for two.

Tune into your heart space and body as you do this, and feel for the result of the calm you seek.

Once you have settled into your body and have inner calmness, create a safe space in your mind. It can be a garden, the beach, the top of a mountain, a special room, or anywhere else that feels safe, secure, calm and serene. This sanctuary is one you can use in any meditation, or when you need an anchor within yourself when things become externally tumultuous.

Once you've created and settled into your sanctuary, call in your inner support team - the best friend, wise person and encourager. These may be multiple beings or energies, or only a single one which encompasses all aspects. Whatever it is, trust that your subconscious and Super Conscious mind knows/feels/sees what is right for you!

Then ask them the questions you need help to find answers to.

Ask them your next best step forward, your next best move, whether you need to move at all, or any other question that you need guidance with.

The answers will always be filled with love, firmness and encouragement. Remember that true, unconditional love isn't always what we want to hear and be placated by. Sometimes we really need to hear the tough answers. Know they will deliver them with love.

Once you have your answer, thank them for their love and guidance, and say goodbye.

You can take time to journal afterwards if you feel inclined.

Exercise: Monitor your Internal Voice

Catch your thoughts as they arise and notice the voice you are using:

Is it kind?
Is it loving?
Is it critical?

What body language is behind the talk (finger pointing, hands on hips, leaning forward, receptive or unreceptive)?
What is the emotion behind the voice?

At times we can recognise influential people from the past in our inner voice. Ask yourself where this particular criticism comes from.

Is it true? (i.e., Is it true that I'm stupid?)
Is it 100% true? (No. I get through most days pretty well, I can tie my shoes, drive a car, operate reasonably successfully in life.)
How can I make this criticism into something uncritical and absolutely true for me? (I did something that was less than ideal because I was distracted.)

Flip the thoughts and comments around:

'I did something I'm not happy about but it's not going to affect my whole day.'

'I'm pretty intelligent, this was because I wasn't fully present and paying attention.'

'In Service To' versus 'Of Service To'

Gritty, real self-love needs us to look, feel and discern deeply around the issue of whether we are being *in service to* or *of service to*. Being *in service to* often feels like heavy obligation and responsibility.

Being *in service to* often comes from a place of selflessness. We put ourselves last and treat ourselves as inferior, elevating other people above us and ahead of us in the pecking order. *In service* indicates that we are not involved in equal partnership; it is inequity - a sense of greater than and lesser than in comparison to the other person involved. *In service* to them, we are being in servitude - completely subject, whether physically, mentally or emotionally, to someone we perceive to be more powerful or important. We are on the lookout for what we can do to serve them, and we often do so at the expense of what we need. Energetically, we state that *'You are more important than me'* and *'I don't matter.'*

When we are *of service to* people, we look after our needs. We make sure that our cup is full, that our needs are taken care of, and we are giving to other people from our excess overflow. Being *of service* allows us to give from a place of equality, self-fullness, and of spiritual purpose. In an *of service* state of being, we have a sense of achievement, we know that we are in support of others, but not to our detriment and not from the role of rescuer. We are able to lean on the other in tough times, but don't feel the need to carry them or sacrifice ourselves for their happiness and benefit.

Feeling *in service* can often be where relationships start to get messy and muddled. Our boundaries get crossed and our needs are brushed aside. Resentment creeps in, as does the tiredness that comes from an empty cup.

It may feel like a soul-deep tiredness, but the soul never gets tired.

What we feel is a nervous system tiredness where our muscles ache, we feel we are running on fumes, and we are heavy, listless and unmotivated. Our stress responses are on high alert, expecting danger if we do not serve.

It can be hard to remember the difference between *in service* and *of service* when life gets busy and you're picked up and carried away at warp speed. But your body and soul *will* give you clues when you've given too much of yourself and are putting yourself further and further down the list of importance.

Being of service is like the rising tide that raises all the boats. There is no better than, worse than, inequity, inferior, superior... It just is. Everybody, including us, benefits from that giving.

Glennon Doyle's podcast *We Can Do Hard Things*, mentions that, when they speak to their children, they often say:

Disappoint as many people as you need, and their expectations of you, so as to make yourself happy and not disappoint yourself.

I ask you to give yourself that permission.

This is one that I struggle with, but am working to improve within my life.

Many times we get stuck in service because our inner rescuer gets involved, along with that not good enough part of ourselves, and we bust our arse to really make a difference in their life. Realistically, in that situation, we are only disappointing ourselves. How many people really notice all that we do anyway?

Cultivating Self-compassion, Acceptance and Honesty

When we begin the practice of cultivating self-compassion, acceptance and honesty, it feels like an impassable road forward. We can't see the wood for the trees and, with past conditioning screaming at us not to make headway, we need a certain strength to start the journey.

Being compassionate is one of the few emotional states that you can never have too much of. Every other emotional state can have negative consequences when imbalanced, but compassion speaks for itself and allows room for growth, even when you are not receiving it in return.

Being compassionate is about feeling with, being empathic, and having the ability to sit with others as they process without trying to fix and move them to resolution faster than they are ready. It is about listening, accepting, being wholehearted and seeing the equality within you.

When we give ourselves compassion, we bring in our inner wise person, best friend, and guides. We let them hear us, feel our pain and discomfort, and simply sit with us while we process. The underlying generosity of this is knowing that, in any given moment, we are all doing the best we can.

Some days, we have full access to our toolkit and sail through life without a hitch but, when life gets stressful and we enter our back brain survival stress responses, the key to our toolshed is missing and we are unable to access the full range of tools we usually can under non-stressful conditions.

Acceptance ties into this. When we accept where we are at, what our emotional states are, and that we can't access our keys, we learn to be honest with ourselves about what we can, and can't, control.

Self-honesty can be the hardest one to work with. We all like to kid ourselves about our successes, failures, how far ahead we are, or how far behind we feel we've fallen. We are rarely 100% truthful but, as we go deeper with the work, uncover more of our subconscious patterning, and become happier admitting that we're wrong, the ability to bring honesty into the equation increases and a certain peace enters.

Sometimes, (actually, who am I kidding?) often, shame, embarrassment and guilt appear. They are enemies of compassion, honesty and acceptance because they want someone to be right and another to be wrong. They want inequality, conflict and resolution within old paradigms of operation.

We all have our own shame story - *'I'm not good enough. I'm unworthy. I don't fit in.'* These play out when we feel injured, set upon and hurt. But, if we recognise the triggers and activations that set them off, we are more able to nip them in the bud before they bloom into full flowers. In saying that, I don't think that, however much work we do, we will ever be fully free of our guilt, shame and embarrassment.

It is part of the messiness of humanity; part of the connective nature of interaction. What we can do is learn to recognise when we are in it, and take steps (either through our own practices or with healers and therapists) to move through the next layers of healing to change our vibrational structure and allow greater internal healing.

Energetic Currency + Discernment = Self-Love

One of the integral and lynchpin keys to self-love is discernment. Discernment is an acuteness of judgement or understanding. It is the ability to sift through the information at hand and make a decision. The prefix *'dis-'* means off or away, which means that when you are discerning, you get rid of some of the options available to you through judgement and understanding to leave other choices behind.

Looking at discernment through the lens of self-love, is about using your discernment in your boundary creation and your ability to say 'no' or 'yes' with focussed clarity on the end result you'd like to achieve.

With all your decisions for Self, put your love for Self first and foremost, knowing that everyone you come in contact with benefits from a healthy, happy, vibrant and energetic you.

When you prioritise yourself, it doesn't mean that you become selfish. In fact, it's quite the opposite. Our Self-Fullness comes to the fore. Where giving to others was once a resentment spiral waiting to happen, the giving that comes from Self-Fullness is more powerful, generous and forthcoming. Giving to ourselves is actually the most radical form of love as it says:

I love myself enough to prioritise me so that I have enough left for you.

Discernment grows with practice. It is not something that you can use once and discard, never to be seen again. It is a life skill, a health tool and an energetic saviour.

When we fully engage discernment, we are able to judge and make decisions about who and what gets our energy, and who or what doesn't. Think about those social situations you walk out of feeling exhausted, absolutely spent. That's an example of someone or something stealing your energy, literally sucking the life out of you. Conversely, you may leave a social event feeling more amazing than when you arrived, and wish it never had to end.

Which fills your cup and which doesn't? That decision is discernment.

When we have multiple encounters with the same people, situations and circumstances that drain our energy, we need to decide whether or not it is worth our investment of time and energy.

Would you put money into stocks, shares, crypto or bonds if you were guaranteed to lose money every time you invested? You may try once or twice but, if you continue to sink money into lost causes, you may have a problem. So, why aren't we as discerning with our energetic currency?

We only have so much to give without refilling, recharging and renewing our energetic stores. If they are being drained more than refilled, we go into deficit and head towards burnout, overwhelm, dis-ease and illness. If we are discerning with our energetic bank balance, and choose wise investments, we end up with a savings plan from which we can give to others, donate our time and energy, and become energetic philanthropists.

Discernment is needed in our self-care. There is a fine line between filling our cup and numbing. When we set our intentions clearly before engaging in an activity, and use the previously described giving and receiving equations, we can gain energy from our usually less nourishing behaviours.

Let's use a couple of easy examples.

Imagine going into the kitchen and cutting yourself a slice of chocolate cake. If you do this consciously, you choose the size of the slice, how much you eat, and you enjoy the smell, taste and richness in your mouth. The whole thing can be a delightful ritual of all your senses combined in unison to create a wonderful, cake-filled treat.

Alternatively, you can grab a spoon and dig in, only becoming conscious when you feel bile creep up the back of your throat.

Only one is nourishing and fills our cup.

Think of Netflix the same way. You can consciously choose to watch something - even a whole series - as your downtime after a busy week. You can choose to sit in your favourite spot, with your favourite rituals - tea, blankets or snacks - and revel in the delight of slowing down, recharging and being one with the TV.

Or you can plonk your butt down and only recognise you've entered a Netflix marathon when the on-screen reminder pops up to ask if you're still watching.

Unconscious versus conscious. One nourishes you and helps you feel relaxed, recharged and ready for the next thing; the other keeps you tired, washed out and listless.

Practice with your discernment. Make it a habit.

Take note of your energy levels before, during and after your engagements, then decide whether they were in your best interest. Take inventory of what made you feel energised and what drained you, then try to add more of the energising intentions and actions in your day to day life.

Remember, change doesn't tend to happen as a result of intense bursts. Try incremental, regular and consistent activities that will create an amazing foundation for what you desire in your life.

Relationships

As mentioned earlier, I found relationships of all types to be a challenge. They were 'hard work' according to the societal picture ingrained in me, and overachieving-me was getting an A+ with the 'hardness' of mine. And then it changed. Everything was flipped on its head.

When clients came to my clinic for help with relationships, I saw them being directed by the huge influence of people external to self, rather than the internal truth of their individual desires, needs and wants.

We often create lists of what we want other people to embody and entail in relationships - the old adage of 'tall, dark and handsome', or your personal equivalent. We ask for a good sense of humour, or financial competency. Our list grows with the physical attributes, emotional traits and desires we have for *them* to embody. Gaps in our own life, maybe? Filling some perceived lack in ourselves, who knows? There's certainly no judgement in knowing what you want and welcoming it in with the Laws of the Universe and intentionality.

But....what if we come at it from a different point of view and flip it on its head?

What would happen if we made lists instead of who WE want to be when we show up in our relationships?

How do you want to behave?
What do you want to bring to the relationship?
What have you got to offer?
How do you want to show up when the honeymoon is over and life rolls in with its challenges, joys and rollercoaster of unknowns?

When we turn the tables and embody the qualities we want to offer in our relationships, whether romantic or otherwise, the change is incredible. Starting with ourselves and working outwards with that focus is transformational, and spreads into all areas of our being to bring success and holistic abundance.

It flips traditional structures on their head, and questions what we've been told about what we need in a relationship. We are no longer working on the Jerry Maguire model of *'You complete me'* (insert vomiting noise here). Instead, we are creating a new paradigm where we acknowledge, respect and honour ourselves as full, whole, independent people wishing to create an interdependent relationship with another in openness, equity and reciprocity.

Another point to explore is what being loved looks and feels like to you.

This can give us huge guidance on what we need to receive in order to feel loved and cared for. Give and take in a relationship doesn't always balance out at 50/50 but the average needs to sit in the 60/40 band or the relationship is unequal. If the give and take is recognised, appreciated and felt, then you've got a great balance, but if you are not receiving their offerings or vice versa, there will be an imbalance and the relationship is less likely to succeed.

A client of mine had left their marriage and was back out on the dating scene. They had been on a date and thought the other person was great, although *'It's just that they're not all in'*. But, throughout the previous fifteen-minute discussion, my client said that they weren't ready to be all in, they needed time to gently engage rather than dive in headfirst, as per their previous patterning.

They couldn't see the link to why the person they had attracted was holding back from them and not fully engaged.

Another client was newly back on the scene and had been on a few dates. Good, but not great. When asking what was missing, they noticed that they were attracting similar to what they'd experienced in past relationships. So what were they putting out?

The conversation led to discussions about what they had not yet healed that may be attracting those personas, and what behaviours were a vibrational match either as opposing forces pulling together or similar forces attracting.

We reframed each attraction point into what it meant for, and within, the client, and worked through each of the unhealed aspects. Gradually, the dating picture changed and, although the end result of a life partner has not yet been reached, the people being attracted in are of a different calibre. Purely because their vibrational output reflects within themselves a certainty, surety and congruence which welcomes in someone else who resonates with that.

Our inner work reflects in our outer world and vice versa. Our behaviours around others are great indicators of where we are in our self-development or spiritual journey. Relationships that begin from a standpoint of self-responsibility are the future.

Who do you want to be?
What do you bring?
What unhealed aspects need to be addressed so you can show up as your Truest Self to benefit you first, then the other?

What do you WANT and NEED?

In my first session with a client, once their history is thoroughly explored, the subject changes to what people want and need from their life to improve their health and vitality on all levels.

There are a few main responses:
- Some people look at me with a dumbfounded look. *'What do you mean? What do I want and need?'*
- The second group respond with a huge list of *'don't wants'* that are disguised as *'wants'*
- And the third group have a vague idea of what they may want to welcome into their life as they move forward.

The first group are the majority. Let's face it, we don't often get the opportunity to talk openly about our hopes, dreams, wants and needs with those we love (or anyone for that matter). We are rarely-to-never asked about wonder amongst the busyness of life and the success we neverendingly chase.

Disguising *'don't wants'* as *'wants'* is prevalent in our society. Our predominant language seems to trend towards the negative rather than the positive. Here's some examples and their flip side:

- I don't want to be sick anymore/I want to be vital and healthy
- I don't want to wake up during the night/I want to sleep soundly and wake feeling refreshed
- I don't want to be in pain/I want to move freely and without restriction
- I don't want to be stiff/I want to be flexible and have freedom within my movements
- I don't want to feel negative in my relationships/I want to feel loved, connected and valued
- I'm tired of being the one to always give/I want reciprocal relationships with balance
- I'm tired of always coming last/I want equality and evenness.

There are a million similar examples. Once you start listening to this in yourself and others, it begins to stand out, making that which was once unseen become super clear and visible.

One of my clients started a business. They'd been through divorce and, for the few years, said:

My number one goal in business is to earn enough to break free from child support and tell my ex to shove that money up their arse

On the surface, that sounds like a pretty good thing to aim for. However, when you feel into the energy of that goal, it doesn't have a high vibration. It isn't about building your own success, standing in your own right as a successful business person, or being *of service* to others. It has the energy of revenge, one upmanship and vengefulness. It is fully based in external influence and not internal truth. Clearing the sabotages and beliefs beneath the system allowed their goal to be reframed as:

I choose to be of Divine Service to the Oneness of the Universe

What a transformation!

Suddenly, we've taken lead and transformed it into embodied gold. The focus is on bringing good into the world, spreading love, peace and healing. Serving God. This is empowered; this is ascension frequency; this is god-damn alchemy at it's fucking best.

I can't wait to see their transformation. Resonating on that level can't help but bring clients, abundance and success their way. They are no longer self-focused but Self and mission focused.

The third set of people, those who have a vague idea, tend to have done some healing in the past and are making baby steps forward. But they often get stuck in self-sabotaging patterns and old belief systems that drag their energy backwards.

Their biggest challenge is to raise their vibration to a stage where they can:
- Lean into uncertainty
- Be comfortable to release old patterns of behaviour and drop their stories
- Feel safe in the expanse that stands before them when they have clear vision ahead, without restriction.

It can be scary to release old stories because we've carried them with us in an embodied state for so long that we don't know who we are without that story defining us. Without the ballast, we can feel untethered, free-floating and have complete freedom of direction. There's nobody to please but ourselves, nobody else to prove ourselves to, and expansion beyond our wildest dreams is ahead of us.

When you've not experienced it before, the freedom can feel like a double edged sword that can drive you back into the safe confines of your old life. Holding the tension of releasing old stories and patterns, before jumping into new ones, is a magical and transformative space which brings miracles into your life.

Although it is human nature to do so, you are not rushing to fill the gap with something just to have it filled. Instead, you are granting yourself time to settle and be. Allowing tension to be present, and to build up, attracts answers and Universal sign posts from a Higher Source to fill the gaps.

Keep asking yourself, *'What do I want and need in my life?'* And don't forget the REALLY important things like:

I need to be loved
I need to be respected
I need money
I need a roof over my head
I need a creative outlet

Work on any resistance you feel when you think through the above because worthiness may come into play and talk you out of admitting some of those needs. They are basic human requirements and it is ok to need them in your life.

For me, 'needs' are survival type, non-negotiable requirements, whereas 'wants' encompass our desires and dreams. Both are ok. You are worthy of both and it is your birthright to admit this to yourself and work to raise your vibration to attract those things into your life.

Journal Prompts

What did you love to do as a child that you no longer do?

What do you need in your life to be content, happy and prosperous?

What does your heart want? What does your soul yearn for?

Who are you when you are alone with your thoughts?

What excites you and creates light and joy in your life?

Balancing Opposing Principles

I will set some context before you fully dive into this section. Masculine and Feminine principles are not related to gender divisions. They have nothing to do with our sexuality, cultural conditioning or gender identification. It is about the balance of Yin and Yang, the Shiva and Shakti, the Divine Masculine and Divine Feminine unity of consciousness. While the idea of spirituality is to move closer to living in a state of non-duality where opposites live in harmony without separation, our human form recognises duality and the state of opposites. Therefore, right now, this is the only language available to describe and understand these principles in action.

The Masculine and Feminine principles are not separate principles. They are one and the same, simply different expressions, like the two sides of a coin. Inextricably linked and inseparable, they express themselves in different ways. We can balance these forces within us to experience greater wholeness and harmony.

We are all a mix of the Masculine and Feminine. The Yin/Yang symbol represents this with two equal halves of darkness and light, each containing part of the other, but both contained within the whole. We are duality made manifest and cannot exist in isolation from the other half of ourselves. We need light and dark, Feminine and Masculine, Divine and human, Spirit and body to be whole, balanced and at peace. They are opposing, yet complementary.

When we think of the Masculine, it is easiest to picture the male sex organs. They are external, projective, giving, penetrative, easily seen, and 'out there' in an obvious way.

In contrast, the Feminine sex organs are hidden, mysterious, receptive, unknown, and only partially seen. To be felt they need to be explored at a deeper, non-surface level.

Therefore, anything that relates to internal movements, emotions and concepts is described as Feminine, and anything that relates to external movements, emotions and concepts is Masculine:
- The outbreath - masculine / The inbreath - feminine
- Giving - masculine / Receiving - feminine
- Containers - masculine / Free-flowing - feminine
- Logic and rationality - masculine / Emotions and flexibility - feminine.

The Masculine principle works with logic, reasoning, control, containers, lightness (the Sun) and giving to others and Self. The Masculine strength is solid and firm, unwavering, and stands its ground.

The Feminine principle works with emotions and feelings, creativity, playfulness, darkness (the Moon) and receptivity from others and Self. Feminine strength is like bamboo, flexible and bending with the intelligence of life, yet unbreakable.

When we are perfectly in balance between our Masculine and Feminine principles we are in union with our spirit, consciousness, and psychological and spiritual wholeness.

We need both aspects within ourselves to fully express the entirety of our being. Too much in either creates imbalance.

This balance is like a swinging pendulum. As we move from extreme to extreme, we are using the energy that we've already built up to carry us into a thought and behavioural position. But, due to the balancing nature of the universe, we ultimately swing back the other way. Think of all the times you've given up drinking, chocolate, or shopping, or started healthy eating plans. You're good for a while, but the pull brings you back into the other side to balance out the equation.

Quite literally, the more we strive for something, the more Universal energy will help you end up with the opposite. The law of attraction, and the way pendulums work, show that the more adverse we are to something, the more we tend to attract it into our lives.

By stepping out of our own way and reducing our striving energy, we change our focus to healthy, life-energy-increasing steps that move us closer to the person we want to become. By using the energy of our future Self, in that moment we can anchor something that's in our Highest Good.

We step out of the swinging pendulum, into presence and nowness.

Being with our decision, and ourselves, in the moment, and surrendering to the balanced forces of the

Universe reduces the pushing, striving, desperate energy within our actions, and allows space for magic, miracle and mystery.

Not many describe the balance between *'doing'* and *'being'*, the Masculine and Feminine, quite like Benjamin Hoff in *The Tao of Pooh*:

Because although Eating Honey was a very good thing to do, there was a moment just before you began to eat it which was better than when you were, but he didn't know what it was called...The honey doesn't taste so good once it is being eaten; the goal doesn't mean so much one it is reached; the reward is not so rewarding once it has been given...But if we add up the spaces between the rewards, we'll come up with quite a bit. And if we add up the rewards and the spaces, then we'll have everything - every minute of the time that we spent.

So, how do we understand the Masculine and Feminine balance within our life and development? Let's work through a few examples.

Goals versus Desires

Goal setting has certainly been encouraged for as long as I remember. Many use the principles of SMART goals - Specific, Measurable, Achievable, Realistic, and Time-bound.

Goals are great, but they don't always take the process far enough to superpower the results. One half of the whole picture, the Masculine state, is often prioritised within each of the working parameters. But, please don't read this and throw your goals out the window *'That's it, they're fucked, I'm done.'* We can use them as a starting point, add colour, texture and 'oomph' to them, and, with a little tweaking, bring more dimensionality to the end result.

How do we balance the energy of the Divine Feminine with the Masculine energy of goals?
Spend a moment tapping into the feeling of the word 'goal'.
How does it feel for you?
Heavy or light? Exciting, or a bit emotionless?

There's often a feeling of incompleteness when setting goals. It can feel like another *'should'* to achieve, another external value to pin our success to, another time to ignore your internal desire and look for external influence with socially appropriate goals. As such, many goals slip into the past, just like New Year's resolutions forgotten by lunchtime on New Year's Day.

Sometimes, we work towards goals that are not what we truly desire. They are what we think we 'should' achieve, what others want for us, or they don't fill us with excitement.

Another problem is that as soon as we've achieved a goal we tick it off the list and move onto the next goal before our pen has even completed the tick. As we tick our boxes, we move on. Never stopping to celebrate, enjoy the moment, or revel in the delight of our achievements. We constantly look for the bigger, better, more, in everything we aim to achieve.

We get stuck in the happiness of pursuit rather than the pursuit of happiness.

Let's use the relationship goals we make, and questions we are asked, as an example. You meet someone and date for a while, then you hear *'When are you getting engaged?'* Get engaged, then it's *'When will you get married?'* and *'When will you have a baby?'* Then, when you have one child, you're asked *'When will you have your second?'*

It's a tiresome, never ending pursuit of a societally-appropriate happiness. You'll be happy when you reach that next milestone, tick box, 'natural' step. But who is that step 'natural' for? Either through our own ideals, or other people's projected ideals, we constantly chase the next thing that will create happiness. We pursue ever illusive pots of gold, believing *'When I get that, I'll be happy.'*

What if that premise keeps us miserable?
What if we turn that around and look for happiness in each moment?
What if we enjoy where we are, right now, and celebrate that with gusto, before moving on to the next thing?

When we balance Masculine and Feminine principles within our 'goal-setting', we supercharge the process. We bring in deeper excitement, and a feeling of fulfilment, not just completion.

How do the words 'intentions', 'desires', 'dreams' and 'visions' compare to the word 'goals'? Goals can feel heavier, full of expectation, and way less exciting.

Desire, intention, dream and vision, feel more expansive, exciting, sexy, and full of possibility. It feels like there's room for magic and mystery to enter when we expand our goals to include intention and vision.

When I think about what I desire in life, I can feel my sacral chakra open and get involved with the process. Our sacral chakra is the home of our sexuality and creativity; the two are inextricably linked. The seeds contained in our sex organs, metaphysically also represent the seeds of our creativity, passions, and our purpose. It is how we birth new creative ideas into manifest reality and bring ideas into form. The creative process is like the process of growing a baby - the idea comes to us, we fertilise and nourish it, then we help it grow, mature and develop into a larger form until it is ready to be birthed into the world.

The balance between goals, intention and vision comes when we set what we'd like our end result to be, and ask the Universe and our Spirit Team for *'this or better'*. This acknowledges that our limited human brain only knows what it knows, and doesn't know what it doesn't know. It gives room for something better than we could have imagined to come in with perfect, Divine Timing.

The Universe is unlimited, so why would we want to limit our results? Endless possibilities of greatness could enter our life, and we could soar to unimaginable heights if we stopped thinking we knew everything, and allowed some magic to enter by giving ourselves permission to relinquish the perceived control we have over our lives.

Time limits can be another restriction with goals. Sometimes, having a date to achieve something is necessary to build a container within which we can create. It can give focus and direction to the creativity flow, allowing it to channel through into reality from imagination and source.

This book is an amazing example of this. After working with my coach for a while, I was asked to have my full manuscript completed and in my hands by the end of 2021. In one form or another, this book has been floating in my consciousness for around five years. But, without a defined date, it would never have left my head to appear in your hands. With the date, the container was set for my creativity to be let loose and appear in manifest form.

At other times, dates can hinder the process. Who's to say that in setting a date a year down the track, we aren't limiting ourselves because our goal could have been achieved much sooner? Or, maybe, the Divine Timing is such that there are other things our soul needs to manifest before we achieve the goal, and the timing of the date we set is, therefore, not in alignment.

When goal, intention and vision setting for your future, tap into the emotions you will feel once you have achieved your goal.

What will happen for you once it is in your life?
Will you feel proud of your achievements, excited at facing the next new step, more confident and creative?

For each goal, I suggest nutting out around four-six emotions that you feel into when you work with the goal. Then continue to tap into that end result, over and over, until you have brought the goal to manifest reality. Within goal setting we need discernment.

Do we need a container of time, or space to allow Divine Timing to play its part?
Do we need to lean more into the masculine or the feminine?

Use your whole body to tap into, feel, see, hear, give texture, colour, depth and full body awareness to your goals. Then if they sit well and feel amazing, keep putting the energy into them until they appear in your life.

The more senses we use to place our order of desire in the Universe, the more aligned your energy will be and the quicker it will be delivered.

Remember that life is about continuous improvement rather than completion of goals. Not everything can be done in a 21 Day Challenge. It is about creating habits, behaviours and goals which generate small steps forward every day, building gradually to lead you to Quantum leaps ahead in your life, love and abundance.

As our inner world becomes more honest, honed and truth seeking, we naturally orient ourselves towards our desires and dreams, and leave behind the hustle and striving of goal-seeking. With a new orientation and a focus on the dreams, desires and excitement that go with it, holistic abundance flows as a side effect - more nourishing relationships, greater financial success, increased health, and more.

Giving and Receiving

Let's now put the Masculine and Feminine principles into the realm of 'giving versus receiving'. When we are in a state of giving, we are fully in control and deeply in our Masculine self. We choose what and how much to give, when to give it; we are in control of the whole process - except for how the person we are giving to receives it.

When we are the one receiving, we are not in control of anything. We don't choose what or how much we receive, when we receive it or how it is given. We are only in control of our reaction when we receive.

This lack of control makes many people uncertain.

When you give or receive a compliment, do you squirm, feel uncomfortable or shy away?

Mostly, this is a reflection of a deep need to be in control to feel safe. With greater internal work, giving and receiving becomes a more comfortable practice.

When you give and receive equally and with balance, you honour both the Feminine and Masculine within you. You allow the Masculine to give and be projective and penetrative, and the Feminine to be receptive, soft and accepting. There is a harmony, peace and ease to the process. It superpowers both sides of the equation.

When someone receives something with grace, how amazing does it make the giver feel? Likewise, when someone's giving is rejected because of our inability to receive, are we stealing their joy in giving to us?

Begin this practice with things that you give yourself, and notice the difference in your energy levels. Start simple and build up.

Before you make your morning coffee (or beverage of choice), think about giving yourself the gift of that hot, steaming, fragrant coffee. Make it with a feeling of love and care, like you were about to serve it to someone you deeply love (which you are, by the way). Whilst in the process of making it, think about how wonderful it will be to take the sips, fully taste and smell it, and mindfully receive it into your body. Give it thanks for allowing you to feel nourished and nurtured as you ingest it. Once the cup is finished, rate your energy, having both given and received the full nurturing and nourishment for that drink.

This works with any other activity. Before you start, acknowledge what you are giving to yourself and set the intention to receive the full nourishment, nurturing and benefits from the activity you've chosen. You'll feel like you've filled your cup with so much more than if you had entered into the activity without intentionality.

However you do it, you need both to operate in harmony and be fully present. We cannot live entirely in our Masculine, nor fully in our Feminine - we need both to be existent to maintain balance and life expression.

The right hand side of the body and left brain are linked to Masculine expression; the left hand side of the body and right brain are linked to Feminine expression. The two halves of our bodies mimic the Yin/Yang symbol - a small piece of the one in the larger dominance of the other and two equal halves creating a whole. The macro world in our micro world is reflected perfectly.

Becoming intimate with our own internal Masculine and Feminine balance is a vital part of spiritual growth.

I was once taken into a meditation with my mentor to meet my internal Divine Masculine and Feminine principles.

My Feminine was a Wonder Woman type Amazon with strength, power, receptivity and kick-ass awesomeness. She was fierce and wise, soft yet strong, a paradox within herself. Oh my goodness - talk about a girl crush!

Then I turned to my Divine Masculine. He looked like Danny DeVito as the Penguin in Batman. He was short, small, stunted and angry. I was shocked.

Before my spiritual awakening, my Feminine Self had been repressed heavily and had almost no voice. In life, she fought hard to control what little she could. She was manipulative and reactive as she operated deeply within her shadow and immature self. I had worked my arse off to bring her out and develop her qualities in the light. But I realised that I had spent so long nurturing and nourishing her that she had taken over completely, and was diminishing the importance of my Divine Masculine. There was no balance. He needed to be heard. He wanted and needed to honour her and she, him. As they turned and gave their messages to each other, conveying what they needed to heal, I saw them merge together and become the two ladder supports of a single DNA strand.

Balance is vital. 'Wholing' means remembering to work with and integrate all aspects of you, without ignoring the hard to love, difficult to understand, less desirable aspects. We need to love the light and the dark, Masculine and Feminine.

Exercise: Meet your Masculine and Feminine

Start by settling yourself into a meditative position - sit or lie down quietly, close your eyes and breathe into your belly.

Once you feel deeply in tune, ask your Divine Masculine and Divine Feminine aspects to come and stand in front of you.

Notice how they are interacting or standing.
Are they touching?
Are they far apart?
Can you see them in the same scene together?
Are they facing each other?
Are they turned away from each other?

What does their body language say about their relationship?
Is it unequal or balanced?
Are they friendly and cooperative or at odds with one another?

What messages do you get about their relationship from their body language and interaction?

Then, ask them to turn towards one another.
Is there resistance or are they happy to do it?
What do they need from the other to be happy turning toward the other and being receptive to them?
Do they need safety?
Do they need to be seen, heard or understood?

Once they are comfortable facing one another ask them to hold hands and look into the other's eyes.
What message does each need to give the other to heal their relationship?
What do they need from the other?
What would make them able to be a team, two halves of a whole?

Note how they interact now that they've received the messages from one another.

Is there anything else they need from the other or from you to facilitate growth, connection and unity between them?

Slowly come back to the room, fully conscious, and journal if you feel inclined.

Holding the Tension of Opposite Forces

*Do you have the patience to wait
Till your mud settles and the water is clear?
Can you remain unmoving
Till the right action arises by itself?*
- Lao Tzu -

Although I am deeply engaged in this practice, and have some pretty profound experience, I still feel like a newborn foal who hasn't quite found its legs.

'Holding the tension' is a hugely important spiritual concept, one that requires dedication and consistency to improve. Maintaining the tension is where the magic is. As human beings, we are wired to want safety, certainty and everything laid out before us - a clear path of step-by-step guidance, a recipe for success and growth, and an end result that is comfortable and relieving in its blandness.

When faced with tension, our nature as humans is to move towards resolution as soon as we are able to.

Nobody enjoys being in a tense standoff, whether in an argument or a life situation with no answers. When conflict or tension arises, we immediately fall into old habits, access deeply ingrained neural pathways, and react as per our 'normal'.

We want the conflict and tension to be resolved and how we resolve it is less important than getting the damn problem resolved.

Many people who say they are averse to conflict are not actually avoiding the conflict itself, but the feeling of tension that arises in the lead up, during, and until resolution. The desire to avoid tension is so strong that people ignore their own wants and needs, deny their own voice, and submit to those who are more powerful over and over again. They diminish their own internal needs and wants in the process.

If we look at conflict with others as a conversation where the end goal is either a greater acceptance or perhaps an understanding of the other, the whole process becomes more comfortable in its discomfort. Our journey through the scratchiness becomes a necessary path to get to that acceptance and end goal.

Tension wants a resolution.

So, if we defy and rebel against the resolution, we create energetic space that wants and needs to be filled. When we sit in the space of tension and allow it to be, we leave space for something else to come in - Universal guidance, creativity, new behaviours and responses, and magical resolutions we may never have experienced before.

How do we do this in practice?

We need to allow ourselves to be in a place of observation, present to what's going on but not emotionally activated and heightened. As we feel the discomfort rise up, it can be enough to acknowledge and validate its existence, and know that it's ok to feel uncomfortable. Give the feeling reassurance and let it know that it's for its own good. And then, we wait.

The waiting is the challenge. We are so used to 'doing', 'forcing', 'striving' and 'controlling' things into action that when we embrace 'being', 'non-action' and 'waiting', we notice impatience and restlessness enter as they try to force our hand.

And then the magic strikes.

Something will drop into our awareness that we hadn't noticed before. We receive a sign - a phone call, message, something relevant - that helps us answer our dilemma in a way that is outside our previous realm of possibility. New paradigms enter, new possibilities, new solutions.

Living the Spiritual Paradox

The hardest thing about spiritual growth and walking the spiritual path is becoming familiar and comfortable in living with, discovering, and accepting, the multitude of paradoxes that exist in our lives. I've mentioned paradoxes before, but I feel they need a deep understanding to allow ourselves to fully engage in life and all its mystery.

This is where we fully and completely live into the *'both/and'* integration of the world, rather than the *'either/or'* duality. We understand that there can be multiple truths in any situation, and move out of pendulum swings into an area of flow and fullness of life.

Carl Jung says:

The paradox is one of our most valuable spiritual possessions…only paradox comes anywhere near to comprehending the fullness of life.

A paradox is the conjunction of opposites, two or more seemingly opposite things being true at the same time.

Spiritual development IS paradox in action.

Even when we look into Masculine and Feminine principles and their expressions, we cannot have one without the other. We cannot operate solely from our Masculine, nor our Feminine. While one may be dominant, they cannot exist in solitude.

Likewise, this is how we give *'The truth has 144 sides'* its full context. Yes, your truth can be true, as can mine. As we look into a situation from our point of view, with our lenses and experience, we own our truth from that perspective. Just as, when we put ourselves into someone else's position, we can see an opposing truth as being true from their perspective. Both can be, and are, true at the same time.

We can also feel into paradoxes with any life situation that involves emotions (big clue, that's all of them). We rarely, if ever, experience only one emotion in solitude. You can feel excitement for an upcoming event, and trepidation at being in a room full of people you are unfamiliar with. At the same time, you could also feel happy at the opportunity to step outside your comfort zone, yet frustrated that you're heading there alone.

There is never only one emotion that fully fits the bill or expresses its presence in a situation. Emotions are often felt in the multiple. And they are all true at the same time.

Think of when your children, or others you love, are pissing you off and being arseholes. You can still hold your love for them while not liking them in that moment. Both are true at the same time because… paradox.

To feel compassion, acceptance and honesty for Self, we need to understand the reality of living in a paradoxical world.

The more comfortable we are with multiple, and sometimes conflicting truths, the greater is our growth and understanding of life.

In this state, it is easier to zoom in and out of situations, which increases our flexibility and ability to cope when situations feel out of balance. Occasionally, we may become too deeply focused on our problems, certain areas of our life, or relationships. When that happens, we need the ability to zoom out for a more wide reaching view of the situation. Then, when we are stuck in the larger, zoomed out picture and need more details, we can adjust our lens and move in.

This flexibility seems easy to manage but, in the midst of struggle and tumultuousness, practicing this skill can be a challenge. The more we practice when things are going well, the easier it is to access when they turn upside down. Pema Chödrön in *When Things Fall Apart: Heart Advice for Difficult Times* says:

The whole right and wrong business really closes us down and makes our world smaller. Wanting situations and relationships to be solid, permanent and graspable obscures the pith of the matter, which is that things are fundamentally groundless.

When we grasp for permanence, certainty, and the duality of right and wrong, yes and no, black and white thinking, we limit ourselves and our experience. If we lean into uncertainty, paradox and impermanence, we grow into expanded consciousness and leap forward into realms we previously only imagined.

The spiritual growth that comes from leaving behind leaden experiences and a desire for certainty knows no bounds.

The gold of opportunity, and the mystery and wonder of life, comes flooding in to create a feeling of deep abundance and gratitude for the lessons, learnings and forward movement that comes with ascension and increased vibrational frequency. Life is one huge messy paradox containing wonder and awe.

Creativity, Humour, and the Spiritual Path

Joseph Campbell wrote:

If you can see your path laid out in front of you step by step, you know it's not your path. Your own path you make with every step you take. That's why it's your path.

You can only see your path clearly when you turn and look behind you. When you look forward, each and every step needs to be forged as you take the steps to create your unique path in the wilderness of life.

Walking a pre-trodden and well-worn path travelled by either one or a whole plethora, clearly indicates that you are on a path that is not made for you.

Many of us follow the paths laid out for us due to expectation, either societal, familial or otherwise learned, but most of us eventually come to a point in our life where we realise that we've been following a false trail, and set out to discover our own soul's journey.

Is it scary to take steps where nobody has gone before?
To clear the path as we walk and have only clear sight when we look back? Of course it is.

This feeling of uncertainty frightens many people. We, as humans, love certainty, control and the power of knowing what's to come. Our true spiritual path is less clear, because it is as unique and individual as we are. It goes against the grain of certainty. It laughs in the face of planning and trying to control your life. But, if we learn to lean into uncertainty, embrace the unknown and bring our sense of humour along for the ride, we can also learn to be a little less scared about what lies ahead. The adventure, playfulness and fun begins to emerge and balance the unravelling of trauma cycles, past hurts, and outdated belief systems.

Creativity is ripe when we are comfortable with uncertainty and the world of paradox. It is easier to tap into our creative flow when contradictions and opposites are able to exist without stealing the energy and focus from our creative pursuits. Being in creative flow increases our access to the full expression of human spirit and connects us to the Divine.

If you're thinking that you don't have a creative bone in your body - STOP IT. We are all creators and have creative energy. Creativity is our life force, our untapped potential. Once we learn to access it, many areas of our life come together with greater harmony and connection, even when they seem unrelated. We are often raised to give little importance to creative pursuits in preference for a focus on intellectual activities and problem solving. As a result, becoming reacquainted with our creativity can fill us with doubt, and bring up belief systems from the depths of our subconscious about the pointlessness of creativity.

When we stifle creativity and stop ourselves from expressing it, blocks are created in the body - predominantly around the sacral and throat chakras. The sacral chakra is where we birth creativity and the throat chakra is used to communicate our creativity with the world.

According to Robert Fritz in *The Path of Least Resistance*,

Problem solving is taking action to have something go away - the problem. Creating is taking action to have something come into being - the creation.

From what we've learned so far, which statement feels more empowering and exciting? Bringing creations into being always gets my vote.

When we tap into creative force we are bringing our imagination and things we envision into manifest reality. What could be better?

If we fall in love with something - an idea, a project, a book we're writing, a painting - creativity is the process from loving it in abstract form to loving it in manifest reality. Another way to think about creativity is that it is our internal emotions expressed into a physical, tangible form that we can see, touch, and feel.

We do, however, need to separate ourselves from the end result. Create, purely for creation's sake and see what you can bring into reality.

Think back to your childhood.

What got your creative juices flowing?
What activities did you love that made time fly?
What experiences absorbed you fully within them?

Our inner child is desperate to reconnect to the freedom, expression and wild abandon they felt when they were in the throes of creativity. Let them out, let them play, let them create.

Another angle to take when you think about what you want and need in your life, is which direction you turn in a bookstore.

What section do you head towards?
What books lure you into them and make you want to pick them up, touch them and flick through the pages?

Look at injecting more of those things in your life and see where they take you. Some may not pack the same punch as they used to, but may whet your inspirational taste buds and start you off on a bread crumb trail towards something that does inspire you.

Remember also that, as young ones, we tried a lot of different activities. Some we liked, some we didn't. Get curious and lean into trying new activities. Visit your local community centre or library, ask your friends, search social media; do whatever you can to open up new experiences and draw inspiration into your life.

As you discover more about what you like, and what piques your creativity, explore more, lean in more, create more. Use it as a springboard for your next pursuit.

∞

Many people think that being on the spiritual journey erodes your sense of humour. That you become serious, more internally focussed and less fun to be around. But that isn't necessarily true.

Often we turn to sarcasm or self-deprecating humour to get laughs and engage in connection with others, but this kind of humour can be cutting and harsh for those who receive it. Often, underlying bitterness comes through as we recognise the internal stories and beliefs beneath the laughs and, for those with empathy, it can create discord when we feel the sadness and insecurity shine through.

Humour is so important on the healing and wholing journey. It isn't about taking things too lightly and not giving them the importance they deserve. (Who decided that 'not taking things seriously enough' was a thing anyway?) It is about releasing pent up old shit that we're carrying in our cells. It is about connecting with our inner child and bringing play and fun into our lives. It is about 'lightening' - literally getting lighter.

So, as you heal, cut yourself some slack, lighten up and have fun. Goodness knows you'll find enough lead to weigh you down! Where you can, bring in laughter, fun, lightness and, if you're like me, a good dose of cussing to the journey.

Because we've just mentioned lightening up, I'm going to touch on enlightenment here. Many spiritual beings think they are either 'way further ahead' or 'way further behind' than they are. We just are where we are, in the given moment. Ahead, behind...actually, none of it counts.

Enlightenment can simply means becoming lighter. Within any healing session, we lose emotional baggage, ballast and weight, so we are working towards becoming lighter. As things shift and change, we see physical changes as we lose the weight of carrying our past trauma.

I worked with an incredible client who had been abused since they were a baby. Some of the things that happened were horrendous, and it was no wonder that they had such self-hatred, low esteem and multiple addictions.

We went back to the moment of conception where they came into the world with a less than loving act. Everything since then reflected that moment. As we shifted the vibrational frequency of how they came to be, this person changed before my eyes. It was like layers of weight dropped away from them, the fog in their aura cleared, and they brightened. They, in that moment, started to enlighten.

When we finished, I told them to head straight to the mirror to look at themselves. They burst into floods of tears and said:

I look like me, but I don't recognise myself. I look completely different.

The immediate change was visceral, noticeable and changed their life.
This is enlightenment in action.
It doesn't always need to be meditating under a bodhi tree, walking on water, or turning water into wine. Yes, Buddha and Jesus were fully enlightened but, for most of us, the journey is about dropping the things that

weigh us down so that we can soar higher than we ever thought we could and become who we are meant to be in this world.

Laugh, lighten, have fun and play. You can heal gently and easily. It doesn't need to be serious business.

Discerning your Soul's Intuitive Whispers

We all have intuitive capabilities. Absolutely every person in this world has access to intuition, psychic senses, and insight. Frequently we close them down, or ignore them, due to our conditioning, past shame, or a lack of understanding of what we are accessing, which can create fear.

When we begin to intentionally tune into our intuition, it is like an unexercised muscle. Atrophying, weak and lacking tone. It takes time, patience and dedication to a practice to build intuitive strength and trust what our intuition tells us.

Throughout life, we are guided to value what the brain thinks over what the body feels, as though bodily wisdom is a second-rate, uncertain way to navigate the human experience. During my early life, until well into the 90s, if not the 2000s and beyond, IQ (Intelligence Quotient) was the highest regarded measure of intelligence. It was easily measurable, comparable to other people, and set apart as THE measure of 'brilliance'. Throughout the past 20 or so years, EQ (Emotional Intelligence) has become a bit of a buzzword, especially in business and leadership circles. But, in terms of measurement, it is hazy and, therefore, put in the 'too hard basket' in terms of celebrating those people to whom that type of intelligence was paramount.

Many of the Beings entering the world during the last 20 years, are now exhibiting a Quantum leap in Spiritual Intelligence (SQ).

These Beings are here to help the planet ascend to new light frequencies and vibrations. To quicken the pace of the alchemy needed to save the environment. To bring love and light into the world, and help us find more harmonious ways of living with nature and her cycles.

While EQ is now more measurable, celebrated and acknowledged than it was in the recent past, in many circles IQ is still the pinnacle that many strive to attain. When you are someone with high EQ or SQ, it can be hard to feel intelligent when IQ is the measure to which most things are compared.

All three types of intelligence are vital for human existence and we need them all to balance humanity in Oneness. We need to celebrate our unique signature of intelligence and find those who balance our strengths to come together in community for the common good.

Seeing the advanced wisdom of children and young adults entering this world shows the rate at which we are ascending. There are a multitude of high vibration Beings coming to elevate this world into something better - they are guiding us into the next Golden Age of civilisation and beyond. A big job, but one they are more than capable of.

Due to the IQ idolisation, we regularly talk loudly over our immeasurable feelings, shout over them at times, belittle their wisdom and ignore the cues they send. More often than not, this path leads us into a place where we can't gain full and complete access to that wise inner knowing that is innate for all of us. If we take the time to befriend it, unbury it from beneath the rubble of our experience, and allow its light to shine brightly, it will guide us in the direction our soul wishes us to travel.

Our soul KNOWS. Our soul understands what lights our internal fires, gets our creative juices flowing, brings us happiness and joy, and lets us become the full embodiment of our Self.

It. Just. Knows.

As a self-confessed word nerd, let me explain the root of the following words - intuition, insight and intimacy - before we head into an explanation about the value of these skills during your alchemical journey. Understanding the words more deeply allows us to anchor them into our embodied experience in an enhanced, more cellular way.

Intuition: direct or immediate cognition, spiritual perception; understanding something without conscious reasoning. This can be further broken down into:

In: not, opposite, without, into, in, on, upon
Tuition: from the Latin, 'tuitonem'; protection, guardianship, looking after, caring for

As you can see from the meaning of intuition, we rely on information coming from senses other than our conscious mind. The conscious mind is limited by what we know already, what we have seen in the world around us, and what we can imagine. The subconscious and Super Conscious (Higher Self) is unlimited. Tapping into only our conscious mind limits us to physical 3D reality, and prevents us from accessing higher, more phenomenal ascension.

When we suspend belief and ask our intentions, goals and visions to be *'this or better'*, we are acknowledging to Universal Source Intelligence that we do not know everything, we do not fully understand what is in our Highest Good, and that we surrender to a Higher Knowing of what could be meant for us. This brings magic and mystery into our lives, rather than consciously thinking with logic and reasoning, and trying to control our outcomes. This practice allows space for miracles to enter.

Insight: sight with eyes of the mind, understanding from within, accurate, deep understanding. Insight is another term which brings in the unknown origin of the thoughts, dreams and magic we wish to manifest in our world. We look deep beneath the surface of our conscious mind and allow the wisdom of Higher Realm energies to make themselves known in our manifest reality.

Intimacy: to impress, make familiar. Intimacy is a huge key in this equation. When we allow intimacy with ourselves, our partners, in relationships, and with our environment, the amplification of enchantment and possibility is out of this world.

Intimacy can be seen another way: **'Into-Me-I-See'**. The deeper into ourselves we see, the deeper within our shadows we are willing to delve, the more we are able to have love and compassion for all aspects of ourselves. With Self-Intimacy, we allow increased intimacy with everyone that appears in our life.

A deep sense of self-intimacy is key to increase and amplify insight and intuition in all areas of our lives. It helps us to set firm, safe and appropriate boundaries, to be open, loving and vulnerable, and to live more wholeheartedly in the world because we honour and respect ourselves in such a Divinely Guided way.

To deeply work with intuition, insight and intimacy, we need to embody our experiences and learnings until they become part of our cellular structure. Real alchemy occurs when we embody our lessons until they become second nature to us.

Embodiment is having the lesson integrate so deeply within our bodily cellular structure that it becomes an integral part of us, physically anchoring itself in our reality. Embodiment is much deeper than a mere logical understanding, and comes from regular practice mixed with trust and faith in something greater.

How do we Access our Insight and Intuition?

Nature and the Universe speak in signs. They don't use normal 3-Dimensional language codes (which are written, spoken and heard in our reality). They speak in feathers and animals and snippets of songs we overhear. Insight and intuition go beyond any language we know. They work in colour, sound, multi-dimensional communication and a knowingness that defies logical reasoning.

We speak to our insight and intuition through our spiritual 'clair' (or psychic) senses. These senses are:

Clairvoyance
Clairaudience
Clairsentience
Claircognizance
Clairgustance and Clairsalience

Remember that we have all of the answers to our questions about what symbols mean to us in our own subconscious mind, if we only care to tap in and access them. When in a meditative or light trance state, we can ask our ego and personality to step aside to allow our subconscious and Super Conscious brilliance to answer our questions.

We are conditioned to *'think before we speak'* and it is one of the hardest pieces of conditioning to overcome when working with intuition and insight. We need to override that conditioning and speak before we think. We learn to acknowledge that the first piece of information that hits our thoughts is, indeed, our subconscious giving us the clues to the internal answers we need. At first, it can sometimes seem that the answer appears from left field but, with practice, questions and curiosity, you'll find you receive clearer and faster communication.

Clairvoyance

Clairvoyance, or 'clear seeing', is receiving messages through your sense of sight. When people think of clairvoyance, many think of seeing spirits and entities, like they do in movies. Clairvoyance is so much more. It can be anything that feels significant to you, that comes through your eyes as receptors. Some examples are:
- Seeing number repetitions - 11:11, 222, 333, etc.
- Seeing animals - bees, dragonflies, magpies, butterflies, ladybugs, etc
- Seeing feathers
- Seeing a specific type of plant or flower
- Having repetitive dreams
- Symbols.

For example, your clairvoyance brings bees into your awareness. You may not have seen bees for a while then, suddenly, you notice bees in pictures, your house, your garden, while on your daily walk, and wherever else you look.

There are a few ways you can decipher the message, so practice to see what works for you. If you choose a 'done for you' approach, search online for *'bee medicine'* or *'metaphysical meaning of bees'* to help you understand what bees mean from other people's perceptions and downloads.

Alternatively, you can feel into what bees mean to you, e.g.,

- Busy - *are you too busy doing stuff or are you procrastinating?*
- Pollinating - *what in your life needs pollination with energy or attention to grow to fruition?*
- Cooperation - *do you need to focus on your role within a community?*

A third option is to drop into a trance or meditative state where you embody the bee, 'be' the bee. You can then ask questions such as:

> *What are you here to tell me?*
> *What message do you bring?*
> *What healing can I do with you?*
> *What is your purpose?*

The bee will then give you direct answers of how they relate to you.

Clairaudience

Clairaudience is the 'clear hearing' of signs from our subconscious, the spirit world and Universal Source. As with clairvoyance, this one can come to you in multiple forms. It could be switching radio stations and catching part of a song with lyrics that resonate or bring you memories from the past. As you pass people on the street, you may catch part of a conversation as they discuss something super relevant to your situation, or a simple phrase may catch your ear and send tingles up your spine.

The other way it can come through is by hearing actual voices or messages situated in different parts of the brain, depending on where the message is from. Some people have their clairaudience come in one side or another, others have it drop through their crown chakra into awareness.

My clairaudience often sounds like my voice talking to me, but it comes from just behind my right ear, towards the base of my skull and is deep seated. When I hear spirits, they come as a recognisable voice, such as my Grandpa's when he is nearby for support. However, when I am stuck in my overthinking brain, the thoughts and words come from the frontal lobes of my brain, just behind my forehead, and are less deep. This lets me know that it's not my intuitive brain, but my thinking brain working overtime.

Over time, and with practice, you too will develop an understanding of which messages you receive and from where.

When receiving 'downloads' and 'upgrades' - either physical or spiritual - you may hear a high pitched ringing in your ears. The left indicates spiritual aspects, whereas the right indicates the physical. At one stage, I thought that I had tinnitus because the ringing was so constant and loud. When I mentioned it to my mentor, they laughed and told me about the upgrades. They then taught me that we can control the volume and get the spirit world to either turn the noise up or down. I set a volume control rated 1 to 10. If they desperately need me to pay attention, they can use a 10, in clinic the maximum is a 5, and overnight, it's not allowed over a 3. This is set through intention and conversation with your spiritual guides.

Clairsentience

Clairsentience is feeling intuition, messages or sensations physically within your body. These messages may be tingles, emotions, colours, energy movements, butterflies, or anything visceral. Sometimes it may be that you feel other people's emotions, not just those from the subconscious mind, spirit world, or messages from the Universe.

When I am spot on the money with my intuition, I get tingles up and down my spine and legs or a full body shiver like the feeling my mum used to say was 'someone walking over my grave'.

Claircognizance

Claircognizance is 'clear knowing' whereby you simply 'know' things. They drop into your brain like mail dropping into a letterbox. This was the sense I had most difficulty with - I always wanted to know how I knew and found that I'd use other senses such as clairsentience to back up the knowing and confirm my intuitive guidance.

With practice, I trust this more and, now, act on it unquestioningly.

Clairsaliance and Clairgustance

This is where you get messages from your senses of smell or taste. An example may be smelling tobacco smoke or tasting whiskey and thinking of your grandfather or father who used to smoke or drink whiskey. It may indicate that they are nearby for support and guidance.

By tapping into our psychic senses, we develop a close relationship with our intuition and create a stronger, more accurate, and increasingly trustworthy, bond with the messages we receive.

You may find that you are strongly connected to one or more of your senses, and may also choose to use some to back up the others. I use my clairsentience to support my claircognizance, because 'just knowing things' didn't fit into what I'd been taught about backing up what you know with physical and actual proof. Feelings, sight and hearing felt more definite to me, whereas simply 'knowing' felt airy-fairy. Initially I didn't trust it, like it was laying a trap for me to fall into and look stupid for professing what I thought I knew. It felt like the ultimate way to be caught out for being the stupid, unintelligent woman I'd been told for years that I was.

As a newbie meditator, I remember asking a mentor what was wrong with me because I didn't see what the meditation facilitators were guiding me towards. They were the first person to describe the 'clairs' to me, which was a truly awakening experience because I realised that I 'felt' and 'knew' what they were saying although I couldn't see it.

> *I felt my body move when 'breeze' was discussed.*
> *I felt colours flowing through my body,*
> *although I couldn't see them.*
> *I knew where I was and the messages I received dropped in*
> *through the mail box near my crown chakra.*

If you can't see, use your senses of hearing, feeling, knowing, taste or smell to determine which one is a sense that you intuitively use, tap into, feel intimately connected to, and trust when you get signals.

All the clair senses can be worked on with a mentor to guide you. I do suggest having a spiritual mentor to help you tune in and work on building those intuitive muscles. Everyone works differently with them and experienced mentors can help. In saying that, however, YOU guide yourself on how you work specifically with your own individual signature.

Spirit Guides, Totems and Higher Realm Beings

This next section is dedicated to those of you who have read about Spirit Guides, Totems and other Higher Realm beings in the previous chapters, and wondered what the hell I'm on about.

Within my belief system, and the experiences I have had in my spiritual awakening journey, I have met and worked with many Higher Realm beings. I work with angels, archangels, spirit guides, animal totems and ascended masters. Everyone has heard, at some point, of a Guardian Angel. Someone or something on the other side who looks out for them and guides them through life.

This concept, whether you believe in its truth or not, is one in which I choose to believe. And, I have seen and engaged with my team, so have personal experience that reinforces my belief. Now, whether that is something I've 'made up', or something that is truth in fact, it is my truth in fact.

I am blessed with a main guide and a team that sits around them. From my very first forays into intuitive work I have attracted many animals to my team and work with a lot of animal energy in healing sessions. My connection to the natural world feels right for me. A wedge-tailed eagle is my main spirit animal, I have a rhino who brings grace, dignity and thicker skin, my main guide brings a lioness with her, and there is a white buffalo and a jaguar. They all bring characteristics, lessons, and guidance that is unique to them, and their input and teachings are always profound.

In addition, I bring Archangels into my work, other healers from the spiritual realm, and other beings which I do not recognise, or need to know the origin of, but they are not humans as we know them here on Earth. Just like the animal totems I work with, they all have their unique signature and input in my life, and bring wisdom, healing, and connection in their own way at the perfect time.

When we learn to commune with our guides and utilise their help we are relying on a support network greater than ourself which really helps, especially in difficult times.

I speak to my guides all the time. In the morning, I greet them, and let them know that I am here to be of service to them and bring their Higher Realm vibrations into this world. I ask them to go forth and meet with the spirit teams of my clients so that we are prepped for any sessions. I thank them for their support and give them gratitude and appreciation for the magic they bring to my days. During the day, when synchronicities, magical moments, and other wonders come in, I say a huge thank you and send them love.

Just like a 'normal' relationship with loved ones on Earth, we build the relationship, talk about what's going on in life, commune with them, and love them. I work as hard on maintaining the relationship with my guides as I do in my relationships with my partner, friends, family and others in my life.

If you're new to learning your team, simply start talking to them - out loud or in your head. Use intention, focus and belief that you are being heard. Ask for signs that they are there and around you - feathers, flowers, bees, number repetitions, whatever speaks to you. Then thank them when you receive them.

Introduce yourself, tell them about you, pretend you are on a date and get to know them. Who knows what it will bring in for you? The more I work with them, trust our relationship, and build our connection, the easier it becomes, the more guided I am in life and the more magic comes my way. And, when times get tough as they inevitably do, I know that I have connections supporting me on every level of my being, in the physical and spiritual realms.

If this resonates, or is part of your belief system, practice, play and have fun!

Now for the Dirtiest Word in the Book: Self-Responsibility

Onto the thorniest, toughest part of healing and wholing... If you're faint of heart, or you're not quite ready, I give you permission to skip this bit and come back later when you feel it's right.

Part of the reason Kinesiology and coaching sing to my heart is that they are 'self-responsibility' methods of healing. Practitioners can only take you so far within a session. You will experience your own internal 'A-Ha' moments, create your own links, learn to trust your subconscious guidance, and need to continue the work with home reinforcement, free will choice, and discernment, between sessions. You choose whether or not you put learned practices and tools into daily use, or whether you store them in a tool shed collecting dust, grime, and rusting out.

When we are in pain, nothing feels better than being able to offload that hurt and pain onto others.

By projecting our pain onto them, and blaming them for being the cause, we often hold the belief that:

If I throw this shit onto you, I don't need to deal with it and, therefore, I can sit in blame and project responsibility onto you, leaving you with the work.

When we are sitting in the truth of our heart and soul, we realise that this practice may not be in alignment with our Highest Good and the Truth of our Soul.
When we are too afraid of external influence and shy away from the courage required to follow our path, we hold onto pain and grief for the life we truly want and desire.
This pain and grief needs an outlet. It loves to wallow, blaming others when we do not take the steps and actions required to move forward. We love to defer our decision making to others, so we then have someone to blame when things don't work out as planned. Others, however, often see through this bid for 'advice' and run for the hills knowing what could happen if things go pear shaped.

Self-responsibility can feel like a heavy burden because we often carry negative connotations with the word *'responsibility'*. When we flip the word around, 'responsibility' becomes 'the ability to respond', which gives it a Higher Frequency and vibrational signature. When we do our inner work and become more whole, we own the ability to respond in any situation - good, bad or ugly. Even when we aren't operating to our potential, we carry compassion, honesty, and forgiveness for Self, and are able to learn from our behaviours, words, thoughts and deeds.

Now for the Dirtiest Word in the Book: Self-Responsibility | 177

When we develop the ability to respond, we set about the real work of transforming our lives, Self and wholing.

Self-responsibility brings to our conscious awareness the programming that keeps us tethered to living in an incongruent way. We feel that we need to continue asking for other people's permission to be who we are. Instead, through self-responsibility, we learn to release this programming and shift into a state where we work for the Highest Good of all, knowing that our path is set before us.

On my toughest days, when life was dark and shadowy, I used to tap into the remembrance and knowing that my life is predetermined; it's written in the stars. All I needed to do was take the next action, say the next words, move my body into the next position, and welcome in what comes. Like an actor on set without full awareness of the script knowing that everything was working out and unfolding the way it needed to.

In the *Dare to Lead* podcast conversation between Brené Brown and Simon Sinek on *Infinite Mindsets*, Simon recalls a quote from a podcast he did with Quilen Blackwell that illustrates this perfectly:

Faith is knowing you're on a team even when you don't know who all the players are.

This is where our connection to our Higher Source, Super Conscious, Spirit Guides, Angels, whatever you want to call them, comes in. Trust, have faith, know they are there to support and do the next right thing for you and show you the next best step, the next best action (or non-action).

Every day we have a choice to leave things not meant for us, or abandon ourselves in an effort to hold onto what is in the past. Every moment is a new moment to choose the path in front, what you clear from the wilderness, which direction you move in, and which things add to the tapestry of your life with positive, clear intent.

And sometimes, we need to save ourselves to reclaim our life.

Walking the spiritual path is not always easy. Walking our walk is vital to staying in truth with our soul. We cannot just profess our values, ethics and morals, we need to live them every day with every aspect of our being.

Understanding, however, doesn't need to be part of our growth - even when it comes to other people. Although it is nice to have, we actually only need to have acceptance for where we or other people are, the willingness to see things differently, and the openness to allow possibility into our conscious awareness.

We are responsible for our part in the connections we have with others. We choose whether we ask questions and bring curiosity to our interactions with others. We choose where our boundaries start and end for everyone in our life.

If they don't treat us well, do they really deserve a seat at our table, our energetic output and the full heart and soul that we share with others who have full appreciation for us?

Discernment, discernment, discernment!
Creating a relationship with discernment, and fine tuning it daily, is a vital key to living your best life. It

helps with:
- Boundary setting
- Self-love
- When to say yes
- When you need to say no.

One of the best tools for discerning is to drop into your body, connect to your heart and feel into:

If it's not a Fuck Yes, it's a No.

'Maybes' suck a lot of energy from us because rumination and questioning sit behind the scenes, even when we aren't aware of them. When we become clear on what a full body *'YES'* feels like, we save a lot of energy, gain clarity and direction, and make decisions with alignment. We also need to check whether our *'noes'* are clear *'noes'*, or *'not right nows'*. You will get the same strong response in your physical body.

Learning to feel our answers and then take action on them superpowers our responses. When we operate from a level of alignment and congruence rather than uncertainty and rumination, the clarity acts like a propellant that moves us towards our desires.

Bringing your Work into Grounded Reality

Spiritual practices often work on opening our crown and third eye chakras or 'energy centres'. These spin and vibrate at much higher frequencies and speeds than our lower, denser chakras that anchor and connect us with the Earth. While they feel fun, expansive and magical -

buzzing and whirring in the body, providing feelings of lightness and freedom - to reach the highest heights possible, we also need a tether to Mother Earth.

In our higher frequency when we are stuck in our head, we are connected to spirit, other realms and higher source, yet when we are in lower vibration and stuck in our head, we tend toward overthinking, overwhelm, anxiety and being *'off with the fairies'*. Our frequency and vibration is the language the Universe speaks; when we speak the same language, we get much better results.

Once again, we need to look for balance between the higher and lower frequencies, and anchor into our heart and soul before connecting to both.

When we have strong roots in Mother Earth, we feel safer and more 'held' as we lean into the future, unknowns and presenting fears. The more grounded we are, the more magnificent our wings and the higher we can fly.

Exercise: Connecting to Earth and Heavens

Breathe deeply, pushing the air into the bottom of your lungs.

Feel your belly move in and out.

Tune into your heart and feel it beating.

Push your energy down your legs and into Mother Earth, visualising tree roots that are stable, strong, deep and secure.

Bring Mother Earth's energy up through the roots, up your legs and through your body energising your chakras all the way up to the Crown.

Push your energy out through the top of your Crown in a bright, pearlescent light which connects you to the heavens above.

Bring that energy from the heavens back down into your body through the Crown, energising the chakras on the way down.

Push that energy down through your feet and into the tree roots, returning the energy from the heavens to Mother Earth.

Keep drawing the energy up from Mother Earth and down from the heavens as though you are a battery with two terminals - one flowing up and one flowing down.

What's Next?

You can fail at what you don't want, so you might as well take a chance on doing what you love.
- Jim Carrey -

In this journey of messy humanness, the more we embody and lean into our curiosity and inquisitiveness, the more we grow, evolve and change. The more we learn, the more we often realise what we don't know about humans, their behaviours, spirituality, and life in general. This either encourages our learning and curiosity, a healthy desire to strive towards becoming the best version of ourselves, or it encourages us to stay small, keep our heads down, and soldier on with the path we've decided to walk.

We have free will to follow the path we choose.

This world and the spiritual realm hold no answers. Yet, paradoxically, they hold all the answers. There is no one truth to pin our hopes on. There is no single teacher, modality, or path that will take us to an end point of nirvana here on Earth. If anything, our internal compass is the best guide we have to show us the next best step.

We do have questioning and, by using the tools we develop to do our internal work, we learn to keep questioning the questions, and being inquisitive about what possibilities may exist if we lean into magic, mystery, and the alchemical process. When we befriend and trust the process, our internal, sophisticated, emotional frequencies will guide us where we need to go. They will answer the questions we have, before kicking up new questions to guide the next stage of our path forward.

Simply ask yourself, over and over:

What is the next best thing for me to do?

Sometimes we can't even take one day at a time, let alone look at our one, three, five, or ten year plan. We need to bring our focus up close and personal to what's the next right step, the next best thing that is in our Highest Good. And then we need to take that step forward.

It's true that there is no end point on this path. You don't have a 21 day challenge to be *'enlightened'* and spiritually *'there'*. Instead, create small daily integrations, habits and practices that eventually become second nature. They take you, little by little, closer to where you want to be. Learn to prioritise what loves you back and channel your energy toward life giving, reciprocal things which add to your existence rather than deplete you.

Learn to take small, consistent actions rather than intensive ones. Yes, a 10 day meditation retreat is amazing and great for the soul, but how do you keep tapping into that once it is over, and life becomes busy and stressful again? You need to incorporate self-care, self-love and other practices daily. Every time things get a little crazy, ask yourself,

What would love do in this instance?

Keep coming back to yourself and your internal truth. When external influences flood in to tell you that you aren't 'good enough', 'worthy enough' or 'loveable enough', fall back to the solid footing and know deeply that you are worthy, loveable and perfectly imperfect.

God doesn't make mistakes. And, who are we to tell them that they made one with us? Know deeply, at a cellular level, that whatever Source asks of you, you can, with ease. And when there's not ease, know that the lesson and needed answer will come to send you the ease you crave.

We are highly individual and autonomous beings, and inextricably connected through the oneness of the Universe.

When you realise this and become comfortable with the discomfort of cycles of death and rebirth, paradoxes, ambiguity and uncertainty, you are able to live more freely than before with a greater reliance on your internal truth over external influence. This world exists in both duality, non-duality, and everything in between.

When we can straddle the worlds, we can achieve anything. We are all works in progress, and this work can lead us further than we could ever expect or dream. It provides enormous inner peace and a desire to spread love, acceptance, compassion and healing out into the world, further than ever before.

Expect the unexpected. Be open to magic and miracles. And remember to keep hold of your bricks. They are yours to build the life you desire, don't let those cunts take them from you.

Acknowledgements

To my partner BJ. We found each other later than we'd hoped, but in doing so we have the beauty of recognising that the growth we went through in the years leading up to our meeting has made us what we are. Here's to many more years discovering the wonder of each other.

To my children. I love you both more than I ever could have imagined. I am proud of both of you for the young adults you are and the people you are becoming. You have been vital on my journey and I am grateful for the lessons you teach me.

This book would not have made it without the vital support, belief and encouragement from so many people including friends, teachers, healers and more.

Ruth Fae - for editing this book with love, care and dedication. You've been amazing at responding to my panicked messages, settling my anxiety and calming my fears. Your support through the process has been incredible and I can't wait until our next one!

Clare Blackstock - thank you for understanding my designs as they are in my head and bringing them to life better than I could ever have explained them.

Meirav Dulberg - thank you for helping my online presence with your website design and support.

Ksenia Belova - the personal branding photos you took of me showed not just who I was when you took them but the woman I am still growing into and becoming. You are a fabulous friend and bless me with your effervescence.

Caroline Connor - Thank you for everything. For reading my baby before it went to print, for conversations about everything under the sun and simply for being a fabulous soul sister. I love doing life with you.

Kim Gasperino - Words cannot express my gratitude. Thank you for your level-headed advice, the love, care and compassion you show, for fighting for right in your work and life, and for so much more besides. Thank you for your support and assistance in life.

Indra - You are such a loveable, fancy, funny cunt. A wonderful friend who makes me laugh, slaps some sense in me when needed and helps me see life in a beautifully balanced way. You and Daarch have so often shown me what's possible in love and life - Thank you.

To Sharan, Dee, Nicki, Samantha and Ioanna - You ladies have seen me through some incredible times and I am grateful for your big hearts, your love, your guidance, your wisdom and our laughs. Thank you all for being wonderful additions to my life. I love doing life with you all by my side.

Rachel....I don't even know where to begin. You have been a nurturing mother through so many of my healings, you have held me, taught me, shared your wisdom and given me some of the biggest gifts I've ever received. Thank you feels, and is, too insignificant to cover the extent of my love and gratitude.

Jordie - You were my first! What can I say. Nobody ever forgets their first. I love our off-the-track healings, the inability to follow protocol, the magic you weave and the work you bring into this world as a proud queer and trans human who helps educate me on things I never knew I needed education on - you help me find blinkers I never realised I had.

Ed and all the team at Kinesiology Connection who taught me and supported my studies. Thank you for teaching me, holding me through my study and the healings within the classroom during the toughest years of my life.

To Pip and the Evolve Now team. Thank you for the Life Coaching training and for your in depth, ancient understanding of the Archetypes and their impact on our life. The work has been profoundly life-changing and I am grateful for everything you've taught me.

There are many more people who have impacted my life, learnings and growth who are not listed here. Please know that I love you, am grateful for your love, guidance, lessons, connection and more.

For exercises on developing your psychic senses and abilities, I strongly recommend my good friend and soul sister Ioanna Serpanos' work. She creates valuable tools to assist your psychic and mediumship journey.
www.ioannaserpanos.com

Bibliography and Webography

A Course in Miracles: Combined Volume (2007, The Foundation for Inner Peace)

Barks, Coleman, *The Essential Rumi* (2004, HarperOne)

Brown, Brené, *The Gifts of Imperfection: Let Go of Who You Think You're Supposed to Be and Embrace Who You Are* (2010, Hazelden Publishing)

Brown, Brené, *Daring Greatly: How the Courage to be Vulnerable Transforms the Way We Live, Love, Parent and Lead* (2012, Penguin Random House)

Brown, Brené, *Rising Strong* (2015, Penguin Random House)

Brown, Brené, *Braving the Wilderness: The Quest for True Belonging and the Courage to Stand Alone* (2017, Penguin Random House)

Brown, Brené, *Dare to Lead: Brave Work. Tough Conversations. Whole Hearts* (2018, Penguin Random House)

Cambridge Dictionary - https://dictionary.cambridge.org

Chödrön, Pema, *When Things Fall Apart: Heart Advice for Difficult Times* (1997, Thorsons Classics)

Dale, Cyndi, *Energetic Boundaries: How to Stay Protected and Connected in Work, Love and Life* (2011, Sounds True)

Dispenza, Joe, *Breaking the Habit of Being Yourself: How to Lose Your Mind and Create a New One* (2012, Hay House UK)

Dispenza, Joe, *Becoming Supernatural: How Common People Are Doing the Uncommon* (2017, Hay House UK) and his live tour about that book on October 29, 2018 in Melbourne.

Doyle, Glennon, *Untamed: Stop Pleasing, Start Living* (on Google Play audiobooks)

Fritz, Robert, *The Path of Least Resistance: Learning to Become the Creative Force in Your Own Life* (1984, Fawcett Books)

Hicks, Esther and Jerry, *The Law of Attraction: The Basics of the Teachings of Abraham* (2006, Hay House)

Hoff, Benjamin, *The Tao of Pooh: The Principles of Taoism Demonstrated by Winnie-the-Pooh* (1982, Egmont)

Holy Bible, Authorised King James Version (Collins)

Jung, Carl, https://jungiancenter.org/jung-on-paradox/

Katie, Byron, *Loving What Is: Four Questions That Can Change Your Life* (2002, Rider)

Lipton, Bruce H., *The Biology of Belief: Unleashing the Power of Consciousness, Matter and Miracles* (2015, Hay House)

Luckman, Sol, *Potentiate your DNA: A practical guide to healing and transformation with the Regenetics method* (2011, Crow Rising Transformational Media)

McKusick, Eileen Day, *Tuning the Human Biofield: Healing with Vibrational Sound Therapy* (2014, Healing Arts Press)

National Aeronautics and Space Administration (NASA) https://map.gsfc.nasa.gov/universe/uni_matter.html

Serpanos, Ioanna, *Giving Spirit a Voice: The Mechanics of Mediumship* (2019, Ioanna Serpanos)

Serpanos, Ioanna, *Giving Spirit a Voice: Daily Practice Cards* (2019, Ioanna Serpanos)

Space.com
https://www.space.com/11642-dark-matter-dark-energy-4-percent-universe-panek.html

The Wisdom of Trauma, film produced by Science and Nonduality (SAND), (Distributed by Science and Nonduality (SAND), 2021)

Van Der Kolk, Bessel, *The Body Keeps the Score: Mind, Brain and Body in the Transformation of Trauma* (2014, Penguin Random House)

Whitecloud, William, *The Magician's Way: What it Really Takes to Find Your Treasure* (2004, New World Library)

Whitecloud, William, *Secrets of Natural Success: Five Steps to Unlocking Your Genius* (2019, Animal Dream Publishing)

Zealand, Vadim, *Reality Transurfing: Steps I - V* (2016, CreateSpace Independent Publishing Platform)

Other teachers and authors who have influenced my work:

Neale Donald Walsch
Dr Wayne Dyer
Kaia Ra
Don Miguel Ruiz
Viktor E Frankl
James Redfield
David R. Hawkins
Barbara Ann Brennan
Caroline Myss
Elizabeth Gilbert
Debbie Ford
Susan Cain
Eckhart Tolle
Sharon Blackie
Michael A. Singer
Regena Thomashauer (Mama Gena)
Lynne McTaggart
Clarissa Pinkola Estés
Stephen D. Farmer
And so many more....I'm sure I've forgotten some!

www.ingramcontent.com/pod-product-compliance
Lightning Source LLC
Chambersburg PA
CBHW030255010526
44107CB00053B/1725